"Rose Grant has helped thousands achieve financial success and spiritual happiness through practical application of sound biblical and financial principles regarding money management."

"If you want to live the abundant life God has predestined—this book is for you! GOD'S WAY TO POSSESSING WEALTH will give you biblical principles to help you gain spiritual and financial success."

—*Reverend Kate McVeigh*
Kate McVeigh Ministries, Warren, Michigan

"Rose Grant has put into this book principles that will bless your life. I challenge you to study and apply these concepts to your everyday life. They will make the difference that you need. Your success depends on you! Let these principles help you now! God Bless."

—*Reverend Dr. Stanley L. Scott*
London, England

"This is a helpful, eye opening resource which will broaden the financial awareness for the everyday Christian and allow them to operate at a higher financial level."

—*Pastor Derek V. Clark*
Psalmist Heart Music Company, Memphis, TN

"Everyone who wants to get out of debt and be financially free needs this book! Evangelist Rose Grant's book, GOD'S WAY TO POSSESSING WEALTH, is just the inspiration and motivation needed to live a totally prosperous life. Her words are not just hype–but a real road map to success in the financial arena."

—*Pamela Perry*, Freelance Writer and
President, American Christian Writers, Detroit, MI

II

GOD'S WAY TO POSSESSING WEALTH

The Path to Spiritual and Financial Success

IV

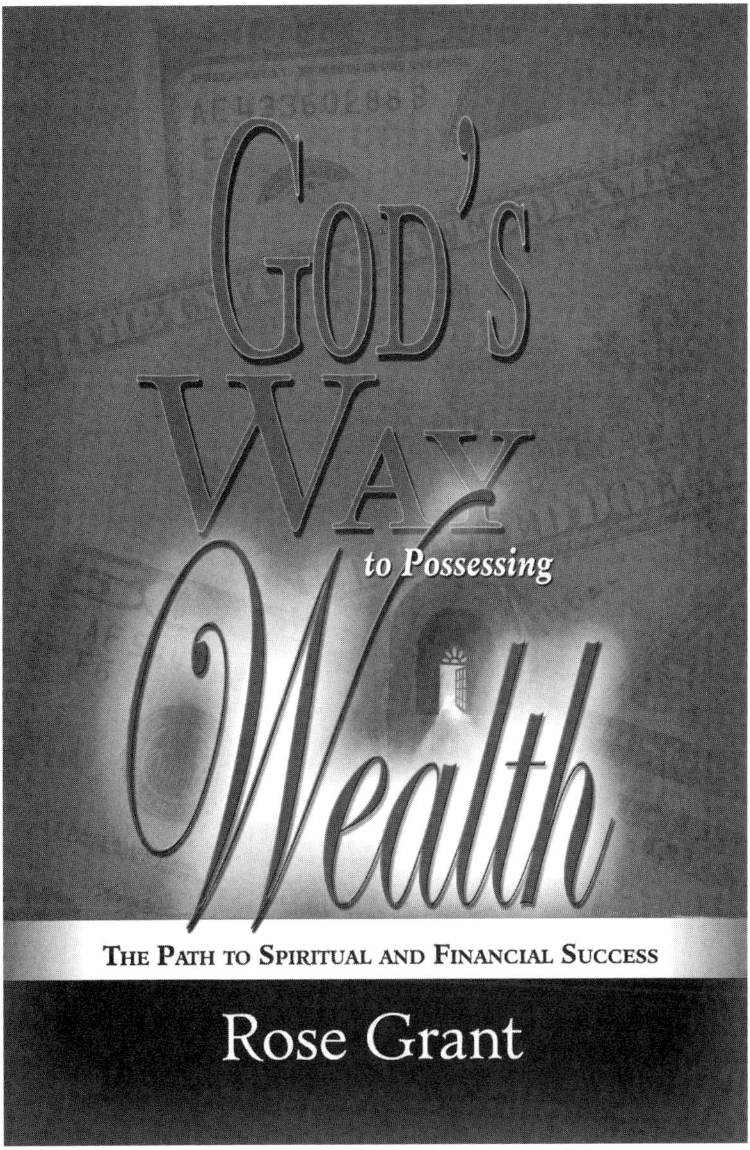

GOD'S WAY

to Possessing

Wealth

THE PATH TO SPIRITUAL AND FINANCIAL SUCCESS

Rose Grant

ROSE GRANT MINISTRIES
DETROIT, MICHIGAN

God's Way To Possessing Wealth
The Path to Spiritual and Financial Success
By Rose Grant
Rose Grant Ministries, Inc.

The information in this book is not intended to be investment and/or legal advice and is not a substitute for professional advice. Readers are encouraged to consult with an investment broker or financial counselor, a tax accountant or the appropriate legal counsel for further information.

All Scripture quotations, unless otherwise stated, are taken from the King James Version of the Bible. Copyright © 1995 by the Zondervan Corporation.

Scripture quotations marked AMP are taken from The Amplified Bible, Old Testament copyright © 1965, 1987 by the Zondervan Corporation. The Amplified New Testament copyright ©1958, 1987 by Lockman Foundation. Used by permission.

Scripture quotations marked NIV are taken from New International Version, Copyright © 1973, 1978, 1984, International Bible Society. Used by permission.

Scripture quotations marked TLB are taken from The Living Bible, Copyright © 1971. Used by permission of Tyndale House Publishers, Inc., Wheaton, IL 60189. All rights reserved.

First Printing 2000 by Rose Grant Ministries, Inc.

Copyright © 2004 by Rose Grant Ministries, Inc.
ISBN: 0-9755081-0-5

Edited by Integrity Editorial Services
Cover and Interior Design by LTerry Design
Printed by Sheridan Books, Inc., Fredericksburg, VA

Contents

VIII

ACKNOWLEDGEMENTS

I thank my Heavenly Father, Jesus Christ my Lord and Savior and my Teacher the Holy Spirit for enabling me, counting me faithful and placing me into the ministry.

To the high priest of our home, my best friend and husband Kyle, thank you for embracing the call of God on my life. Your unconditional love for me, along with your godly wisdom and administrative support has helped make this vision come to pass.

In memory of my loving father Donald A. Drummond, the man with a giving spirit, and to my mom Gwendolyn E. Drummond, thank you for imparting the anointing to prosper into my life. Your ministry of giving is an extraordinary example of "blessed to be a blessing."

To Psalmist Kyla Chere Grant and future NBA All-Star, Kyle Craig (Sauce) Grant II, my wonderful kids. You are the generation of the upright and you shall be blessed!

To my spiritual parents, Bishop Keith and Minister Deborah Butler, Founders of the Word of Faith International Christian Center and Word of Faith Bible Training Center. Thank you for teaching me the uncompromised Word of God. Your obedience to God has made it possible for me to get the training necessary to fulfill the call of God on my life.

To Stacey Hanks my covenant prayer partner and confidante. Thanks for your continuous encouragement and for running with this vision. I appreciate all the times you would "nudge" me saying, "When are you going to get the book done?" I also thank you for your insightful edits and your attention to detail.

Thank you Evangelist Kate McVeigh for your countless prayers and for always telling me "Rose I believe in you. You can do it." I also thank God for the opportunity to serve you.

To my book lover extraordinaire—Pam Perry, your work, prayers and encouragement were not in vain. Words cannot express my deep appreciation for the plethora of information and inspiration you have provided.

To the Reverend Dr. Stanley L. Scott, my Dean and my mentor! Thanks for seeing the hand of God on my life and speaking into my life accordingly. I am moved with tears of gratitude as I reflect on your godly counsel when times were really tough for me. I still remember your quote from your lovely wife Carolyn about making hasty decisions.

A special thank you to Pastor Solomon Turner for prophetically speaking into my life at a critical point when I was deciding whether or not to become a financial planner alongside preaching the gospel. Thanks for telling me to "close the financial planning book and open The Book." To your wife and my dear friend "the lovely LaVita," words cannot express the depth of love I have for you. I thank God for knitting our hearts together in love. Thank you for the words of wisdom and knowledge you have imparted to me.

Last but not least, to LaTanya Terry — words cannot express my gratitude for your seeds sown into my ministry and this project. Your cover design and book layout is awesome! Expect God to Bless you and your family exceeding abundantly above all that you may ask or think.

INTRODUCTION

This book is written to help eradicate a poverty mentality and an attitude of defeat towards wealth and prosperity. My goal is to share techniques and examples that demonstrate God's will for His children to live a super abundant life here in the earth.

For years, many in the Body of Christ have believed that it is a holy act to serve God and live in poverty and lack. There are many people who still believe Christians should not have an abundance of wealth, and that having lots of money is evil. We have been deceived into thinking God's children are not supposed to prosper and walk in the blessings which He preordained for us to experience before the foundations of this earth.

Little by little, we are beginning to receive revelation of God's will for us to prosper and succeed in every facet of our lives. Many are getting revelation of the scripture in 3 John verse 2 where it says, *"Beloved, I wish above all things that thou mayest prosper and be in health, even as thy soul prospereth."*

The writer of this scripture, under the inspiration of the Holy Spirit says, above all things he prays that we may, in all respects, prosper and keep well. To prosper means to succeed, to break out, to go over, and to be profitable. God's desire for us is that we succeed in everything we do—not only financially, but also physically and spiritually.

Can you imagine being so successful that your total tithes for a 12-month period exceed $1 million dollars? I can! Can you imagine having your entire family saved, sanctified, filled with the Holy Spirit and walking strong in the Lord? I can—there is nothing too hard for God!

Fill your imagination with the many promises found in God's Word and begin to see these promises coming to pass in your life. To get more out of life, you must demand more of your imagination. I often say, "what you are today, you first imagined it and then spoke it into existence." As a man thinks in his heart, so is he (Proverbs 23:7). Think about that!

In Genesis Chapter 11, God made a profound statement about the people who came together to build the tower of Babel. He said, "Nothing they imagined they could do, will be impossible for them to do." Although they were building the tower out of disobedience, imagine what God will do when our thought-life lines up with His Word. He will do exceedingly, abundantly above all we ask or think, according to the power that works in us. Here are my questions to you: What have you been thinking in your heart? Moreover, what are you asking God to do?

Repeatedly, we see in God's Word that it is the will of the Father for His children to walk in His blessings above measure. In the original Hebrew text of the Old Testament, to be blessed means: to be happy, fortunate, enviable, to prosper and to have a liberal reservoir. In the original Greek text of the New Testament, to be blessed means: supremely fortunate, to be happy and well off, to confer benefit on and to prosper. God wants you blessed!

Ask yourself these questions: When people observe my life, do they look at me and see that I am supremely fortunate and happy, having a liberal reservoir of all I need? Do they look at me and wish they could live where I live, drive what I drive, wear what I wear, vacation where I vacation and serve the God I serve?

Do they wish their marriages and families could be as successful as my marriage and family? These are profound questions, yet many believers cannot answer in the affirmative—Yes! This state of being saddens your Heavenly Father.

It is your Father's desire to make you a gazing stock for all the people on the earth to look upon and see that you are called of God. In order for the 21st century Church to fully represent the Almighty God, we must have faith with corresponding actions to receive the blessings He has reserved for us.

Due season is here for the Body of Christ! It is time to possess the wealth that has been stored up for us. It is time to take back what is rightfully ours. We have had faith to receive Jesus as Lord of our lives. We have faith to receive healing in our bodies. Now is the time to lift our faith to receive the abundant, God kind of life, which was predestined before the foundations of this earth. It's time to possess God's wealth!

As a child of God, we have the just and legal right to ownership of God's property. God gave man dominion over ALL things in Genesis 1:26. Although Adam forfeited that dominion out of disobedience to God's instruction, Jesus reclaimed that power when He defeated Satan on the cross.

Jesus then transferred that power and dominion to everyone who believes in His name. "And he said unto them (His followers), I beheld Satan as lightening fall from heaven. Behold, I give unto you power to tread on serpents and scorpions, and over all the power of the enemy: and nothing shall by any means hurt you." (Luke 10:18-19)

Jesus told us to occupy, which means to take ownership and to buy and sell things in the earth until He returns (Luke 19:13). Jesus gave us power and dominion over all things, wealth included!

To occupy and take ownership, you need to receive the power to possess the wealth. With that power and authority, believers should be the ones dominating the real estate market. Land is our inheritance. "The earth is the Lord's and the fullness thereof; the world, and they that dwell therein." (Psalm 24:1)

God gave us dominion here in the earth. "The heaven, even the heavens, are the Lord's; but the earth hath he given to the children of men." (Psalm 115:16) The scripture goes on to say in verse 17 that the dead praise not the Lord. This means that God wants us to possess the wealth in the earth before we die.

Those who have made the Lord their God should be the ones dominating the wealth in the earth. We should be the recipients of the wealth transference that is taking place in the earth. We should be the ones investing in the stock market instead of sitting on the sidelines watching the wealth go by.

Although the majority of investors in the stock market are legitimate, many are driven by greed, fear, lying and cheating. It is evident that these are all attributes of the enemy. I believe the initial establishment of the investment markets was "a God idea." However, over the years the notion of investing has been corrupted because there is lack of godly character exemplified by many who currently possess the wealth.

Clearly, Christians are not fulfilling Jesus' command to take ownership until He returns because we are not dominating the wealth in the earth as Jesus commanded us to. It is time for us to possess, preserve and distribute God's wealth.

The time has come for the children of God to rise up and take our position of authority. You must know who you are in Christ Jesus and know what belongs to you. Understand and forget not the benefits that God provides to us daily (Read Psalm 103).

Now is the time for us to walk in the power God has freely given to us. It is our time to demonstrate to the world the goodness of our Heavenly Father. Why demonstrate God's goodness? Because it is the goodness of God that leads men to repentance. (Romans 2:4)

God wants His inheritance. God's inheritance is people saved and delivered from sin. God wants His inheritance just as much as we want Him and His wealth. When we make God rich by leading the lost to our Savior Jesus Christ, He will make us rich by giving us an abundant supply of all we need.

Someone reading this book is going to receive the spirit of Joshua and Caleb—that spirit that believes the wealth of the wicked belongs to the just and now is the time to go up and take possession of the wealth. I believe that the just are well able to do it!

The world must see that God is a faithful God—He is the sustainer of all creation. The set time has come for the children of God to participate in the great wealth transference taking place here in the earth.

Begin to ask God to show you specifically how to possess His wealth that is being held back from you. Begin to set aside quiet time to listen intently to His instructions, then do what He tells you to do and do it now! Do not procrastinate. Stop saying, "I cannot do that." What you are saying you cannot do, someone else has already been there and done that. Only those who take the steps necessary to acquire the wealth will enter into their wealthy place.

I have divided this book into two parts. In Part I, I focus on the spiritual aspects of possessing wealth. I firmly believe that as children of God, we have to do things God's way, and the things of God are first accomplished in the Spirit. In Part II, I share the "nuts and bolts" of money management, with natural applications that have been used successfully by many to attain financial freedom and amass wealth.
As you study the material in this book, I earnestly pray that the God inspired words within will motivate you and change your life as you follow *God's Way to Possessing Wealth.*

PART I

"Therefore if you have not been faithful in the [case of] unrighteous mammon (deceitful riches, money, possessions), who will entrust to you the true riches?"

—*Luke 16:11*

Chapter 1
RESTORATION IN THE LAST DAYS

I earnestly believe we are living in the last days before the imminent return of our Lord and Savior, Jesus Christ. When the Lord Jesus Christ returns for His Church, it will not be in financial ruin, living from paycheck to paycheck; nor will it be in a state of indebtedness. I declare that we are coming out of debt and we will perpetually live debt-free, in the Name of Jesus. The choice is ours.

Scripture tells us that Jesus is coming back for a glorious church without spot or wrinkle. Debt is a spot. Poverty and lack are spots, which cause blemishes and even disgrace. The Church, those who love and serve God, will be without spot or wrinkle. I agree with Ephesians 5:27: *"That He might present it* (the Church) *to Himself a glorious church, not having spot, or wrinkle, or any such thing; but that it* (the Church) *should be holy and without blemish."* The Church will be whole, nothing missing and nothing broken.

I believe that upon Jesus' return, the Body of Christ will be fitly joined together, walking in the full measure of God's covenant promises to bless us physically, spiritually, and financially. Through the shed blood of Jesus and the efficacy that is in God's Word, all things are being restored back to man's original state from where Adam fell into sin.

Before Adam fell, He was in the Garden of Eden—the garden God planted. This garden was a place of paradise, a place of pleasure and delight. In Isaiah 51:3 and Ezekiel 36:35 Eden is illustrated as the great prosperity God would bestow on His people. From the beginning of time, God's intent for His people was that we live in paradise, pleasure and delight—that is, to live in luxury.

Close your eyes and picture yourself living in luxury — experiencing all the beautiful things God has created. Got the picture? Now take that picture with an eye of faith, being firmly persuaded that that's what your Heavenly Father intends for you to have. It's important to know that God has not changed His mind. *God is the same yesterday, today, and forevermore* (Hebrews 13:8)! Our Heavenly Father still intends for His children to live in paradise, pleasure and delight while on the earth.

> "For it is God which worketh in you both to will and to do of His good pleasure."
> —Philippians 2:13

We are living in the days prophesied by the Prophet Joel where God is pouring out His Spirit upon all flesh. Those receiving the outpouring of His Spirit will be able to walk in the overflow of His blessings. In order to receive, you must participate in the outpour. Think about this: If you are pouring water upon someone, you cannot accomplish the pouring out if that someone is far away from you, can you?

In order to be "poured out upon," you must come close to, or at least within arms length to the one who is pouring out. God is the same way. In order for God to pour out His Spirit upon you, you must first come close to Him. He said, "draw near to Me and I will draw near to you." (James 4:8)

You will not receive the outpouring of the Holy Spirit or His power to get wealth if you do not spend time in His presence. You get to know Him more deeply when you become more intimately acquainted with Him; and the way to intimacy with the Lord is through daily thanksgiving, praising, worshiping, studying, meditating, speaking and applying His Word. This is God's way to possessing wealth.

> "But thou shalt remember the Lord thy God: for
> it is He that giveth thee power to get wealth, that He
> may establish His covenant which He swore unto
> thy fathers, as it is this day."
>
> —Deuteronomy 8:18

CHAPTER 2

RECEIVE THE GLORY!

These are the most exciting days in Church History. Many prophets and righteous men have desired to see the things we are seeing; and to hear the things that we are now hearing. As the Lord pours out His Spirit in these last days, we will begin to experience greater revelation, knowledge, and understanding of His Word. As the knowledge of God increases, His glory will increase throughout the world.

The Lord says, "The glory of this latter house (this generation of believers) will be greater than the former (Haggai 2:9)." Hallelujah! This means that His splendor, His goodness, His honor and His manifested presence will be greater for this latter generation of believers than ever before.

I believe God will do greater works through this generation of believers. I believe this generation is the generation of this latter house who will usher in the return of Jesus the Anointed One.
Do you believe? *All things are possible to them who believe* (Mark 9:23). Jesus said because we believe on Him, we will do the works He has done and we shall do greater works (John 14:12)!

We should be seeing and expecting greater miracles in these last days: Miracles of healing. Miracles where we see millions of people accept the gift of salvation. There should be great anticipation for the miraculous to take place in the area of our finances. I dream of the day and time when God's <u>wealth is transferred</u> into the hands of His children!

Jesus did great works before His death, burial, and resurrection. Jesus went about doing a lot of great things during His time of ministry. Jesus expects us to do greater works! We will accomplish greatness once we understand who we are in Christ Jesus. Once we fully understand that the Greater One lives on the inside of us, we too will walk in greatness.

We must let this mind be in us that was also in Christ Jesus, as the Apostle Paul wrote in Philippians Chapter 2. What was the mind of Christ? His mindset was, "I and the Father are one. Because God is, I am. Because God can, I can. Because God said it, that settles it." We too must let this mindset be in us, *knowing that as Jesus is, so are we in the earth* (1 John 4:17).

When you read the Scripture, you must stop and meditate on what the writer is saying. For example, when I read, "As Jesus is," I ask the question, how is Jesus? I see Jesus as very loving, compassionate, all-powerful, miraculous, mighty, and wealthy.
I could go on infinitely about the attributes of Jesus.

God sees you as He sees Jesus. In fact, when God looks at you, He sees the blood of Jesus. The blood of Jesus was sprinkled on the mercy seat for you and I. Whenever God looks at us in our fragile state, He sees the blood of Jesus, which allows Him to have mercy on us. God always sees you at your fullest potential in Him.

> "In Him you live, move and have your being."
> —Acts 17:28

He always sees you as the person He created you to become.

Jesus walked the earth as a man anointed by God. God anointed Him and *He went about doing good and healing all that were oppressed of the devil; for God was with Him* (Acts 10:38). The same anointing that was available to Jesus then, is available to you today. We must believe and do greater works.

> "Jesus said to her (Martha), Did I not tell you and
> promise you that, if you would believe and rely on
> Me, you would see the glory of God?"
> —John 11:40 AMP

Believe that God is able to teach you to profit. Believe that God is able to give you power to get wealth. Believe and expect the glory!

The glory of God is His manifested presence; it is where God makes His presence known. Hungering and thirsting after God makes room for Him to show up and to show us His glory. When the glory comes, everything that is wrong, everything that hinders us, everything that has kept us in bondage, must disappear.

I liken the glory of God to a type of light. Just imagine for a moment, a room full of roaches (poverty, sickness, lack). Yuk! Yuk! When the light comes on, the roaches scatter. Believers have the ultimate light on the inside. Your light has the power to scatter life's burdens. Recognize the light within and let your light shine!

> "The spirit of man is the candle of the Lord, searching
> all the inward parts of the belly."
> —Proverbs 20:27

We activate that inward light when we hunger and thirst after the presence of God. Moses, an Old Testament believer, had a great hunger and thirst for God and as a result, God manifested His glory to the people of Israel many times. In the Old Testament, the glory came and went. God's people were in dire straits (distressed and impoverished) with their backs up against the wall, and they needed a move of God to help them in their distress from being enslaved to Pharaoh. (See Exodus 1-14)

Moses set aside time to seek God for instructions on leading His people from bondage. As long as you seek (yearn for, inquire, search for and research) the Lord, He will make you prosper.
(2 Chronicles 26:5)

What are you bound by today? Is it debt? Is it lack? Is it sickness in your body? Are you lacking joy? Are you lacking peace? No matter what has you bound, even if it is to the point where you cannot see your way out, set yourself to seek the Lord. Ask the Holy Spirit for help. He is your helper and He is a very present help in times of trouble.

When Moses sought God, He showed up. As a result, Moses experienced the glory when the power of God appeared to him in a burning bush. When the power of God parted the Red Sea, that was the glory! When the power of God led the Israelites through the wilderness with a pillar of cloud during the day, and with a pillar of fire by night to give them light, that was the glory!

When manna fell from heaven to feed the Israelites in the wilderness that was the glory! When water gushed out of a rock to quench the thirst of over a million people, that was the glory! Those manifestations of God's glory were good, but the best is yet to come! Are you hungry for more of God?

Thank God! We have a better testament and it is fresh and new! Through the shed blood of Jesus we have a new, better covenant, which was established upon better promises. Because of the new covenant, Christ (The Anointed One and His Anointing) is completely and permanently formed (molded) within you.

It is God's desire to make known to you *the riches of His glory, which is Christ in you, the hope of glory.* (Colossians 1:27) When we allow the Spirit of God, who lives in us, to radiate in and out of us, we will see the glory covering the earth! When we allow the love of Jesus to radiate in and out of us, we will begin to see visible manifestations of the attributes of a God who is holy, righteous, and loving. When we exemplify the character of God in our lives, we make known His glory and His goodness.

The whole earth is travailing like an overdue pregnant woman. The rocks, the trees, all creation are travailing to see the manifestation of the sons of God. (Romans 8:19) The level of glory we have never seen before will come when the sons of God manifest the love and power of our living God! Manifestation of God's glory brings manifestation of God's wealth.

God manifested Himself when Jesus instructed Peter to go to the sea, cast out a hook, and take up the first fish that came up.

> "Open the mouth of the fish and you will find a piece of money."
>
> —Matthew 17:27

Praise God for supernatural increase—miracle money out of the mouth of the fish. You may say "Ah! That only happened in biblical days." Can I tell you that God will never run out of miracles? He is still a miracle worker.

I believe one of the greatest miracles we are about to see in the earth is the transference of wealth into the hands of God's trustworthy people. God has to be able to trust you with the wealth. When you become faithful over little, He will make you ruler over much. When you use wisdom and when you become a good steward over the money you have now, God will give you more and more.

When the transference comes, we will begin to usher in the second coming of our Lord and Savior Jesus Christ. Why do I believe this? When the wealth is in the hands of God's faithful stewards, they will appropriate the wealth to fund the preaching of the Gospel. The Gospel will exponentially spread throughout the four corners of the world because God's people will dominate the financial supply.

> "And this gospel of the kingdom shall be preached
> in all the world for a witness unto all nations; and
> then shall the end come."
> —Matthew 24:14

I am here to tell you—God is still in the business of working miracles. He desires now more than ever to show you His glory in every facet of your life! You must, however, seek after Him like a thirsty soul in a dry land where there is no water. You must seek and wholly follow the Lord in order to see His power and His glory manifest in your life. God said,

> "He rewards those who diligently seek Him."
> —Hebrews 11:6

> "...The glory of the Lord shall be thy reward."
> —Isaiah 58:8

When the world sees God's prosperity, God's favor, His love and the outpouring of His miracles upon His children, all the people of the earth shall see that we are called by the name of the Lord. I believe people all over the world will begin to call on the name of Jesus. Every nation, power and tongue will recognize Jesus is Lord to the glory of God. They will ask, "What must I do to be saved?" Hallelujah!

Sheba

"But as truly as I live, all the earth shall be filled with
the glory of the Lord."

—Numbers 14:21

HE DID IT BEFORE

He did it before and He will do it again! In the book of Nehemiah,
we see a group of believers returning to God after they had fallen
away from Him. In Nehemiah chapter 5 verse 11, God commands,
*"Restore, I pray you, to them, even this day, their lands, their vineyards,
their olive yards, and their houses, also the hundredth part of the money,
and of the corn, the wine, and the oil, that ye exact of them."*

If you study this out in the original Hebrew text, God is literally
saying, "give back to them (His children) this very day their
fields and their houses. And pardon the debts of money which you
have lent them and drop your claims against them!" Oh! That's
shouting news!

In this scripture, I see the children of God possessing stored up wealth.
I also see debt cancellation. Glory to God! What did these people
have to do in order to receive the blessings of God? They returned
to and pressed into God. They began to do as He commanded in His
Word.

The Lord said if we walk in His statutes, and keep His commandments and do them, He would rain increase upon us.

> "I will be leaning toward you with favor and regard you
> rendering you fruitful, multiplying you and establishing
> and ratifying My covenant with you. And you shall eat
> the [abundant] old store of produce long kept, and clear
> out the old [to make room] for the new."
>
> —Leviticus 26:9-10 AMP

It's time for the new. It's a new season, beloved. It is a suddenly season! Suddenly, God is going to rain increase on those who keep His commandments. It is due season for those who have been faithful in keeping God's Word. The set time has come for God to favor you!

> "You will arise and have mercy and loving-kindness for Zion (the Church), for it is time to have pity and compassion for her; yes, the set time has come [the moment designated]."
>
> —Psalm 102:13 AMP

God said He changes not. There is no variableness with Him. In other words, God is no respecter of persons—He does not exhibit partiality. He is however, a respecter of faith. Because He restored the Old Testament believers who turned to Him in faith, how much more should He do the same for the faith-filled New Testament believers? What He has done for others, He will do for you. You must have faith and put your trust in God.

> "Jesus Christ the same yesterday, and today, and for ever."
>
> —Hebrews 13:8

CHAPTER 3
HE RESTORES MY SOUL

In order for you to receive the precious promise of restoration of God's wealth, you must first allow God to restore your soul. Restoration of your soul entails a transformation of your:

Mind — your intellect, your ability to reason
Will — your determination, your choices
Emotions — what you feel, what moves you to do what you do

Your will must line up with God's will. In order for this to take place, you must know God's Word. God's Word is His will. Your mind, will and emotions will become transformed and be renewed as you read, study and meditate on the Word of God.

Once your mind is renewed, you must understand God's plan and His original purpose for restoring you in every area of your life. God wants to restore your soul simply because He loves you and He desires to fulfill all that He has promised you.

It is important for you to recognize however, that a fool with an abundance of wealth is likened to a one-year-old baby with a loaded gun—dangerous! The Word of God clearly shows that *the prosperity of fools shall destroy them* (Proverbs 1:32). To avoid foolishness and destruction, you will need transformation, godly counsel, wisdom and understanding. You must prepare to be restored because transformation comes before restoration.

> "I appeal to you therefore, brethren, and beg of you in
> view of [all] the mercies of God, to make a decisive
> dedication of your bodies [presenting all your
> members and faculties] as a living sacrifice, holy
> (devoted, consecrated) and well pleasing to God,
> which is your reasonable (rational, intelligent)
> service and spiritual worship. Do not be
> conformed to this world (this age), [fashioned after
> and adapted to its external, superficial customs],
> but be transformed (changed) by the [entire]
> renewal of your mind [by its new ideals and
> its new attitude], so that you may prove [for
> yourselves] what is the good and acceptable and
> perfect will of God, even the thing which is
> good and acceptable and perfect [in His sight
> for you]."
>
> —Romans 12:1, 2 AMP

It is time out for child's play. We must not conform to the world's way of living. We must be transformed into God's way that leads to abundant life. As believers in the earth, we must walk in our God-given authority. We must get in position to allow God's light to shine through us before men in order for them to see our good works and glorify our Father which is in heaven.

It is time to show the world that it is the goodness of God that leads man to repentance. You show God's goodness when you are walking in prosperity, peace, and wholeness; where there is nothing missing and nothing broken. The world is waiting for you to demonstrate your position of authority. They need to see the resurrection power of Jesus coming out of you.

The same power that raised Jesus from the dead resides in you. Pause and calmly think about that. When you realize that the Greater One lives inside you and that you are more than a conqueror, you will then come to a full understanding that there is nothing too hard for God. Perhaps at that point, you will begin to walk in your God-given authority. God is waiting on the Body of Christ to exercise her authority!

Where are the sons of God who will allow their image to be fully transformed into His image, whereby God will manifest Himself in such a way that the whole creation will stand in awe when they see the awesome blessings God pours upon them? (Romans 8:19)

The world is waiting to see that which they have never seen before. They need to see the institution of marriage being restored to the fullness of agape (God-kind of unconditional) love.

The world needs to see the prosperity of God's people. They need to see sickness and disease in flight. They need to see the reconstitution or the return of things stolen from the sons of God. The earth is the Lord's and the fullness thereof. The wealth belongs to our Father. He created the wealth for His children to enjoy, not for Satan's disciples to enjoy. It is time to bring our Father pleasure. God takes pleasure in the prosperity of His servant (Psalm 35:27). This is an Old Testament promise. We are no longer servants. We are sons of God. How much more does He take pleasure in our prosperity?

When those who are lost (out of fellowship with God) begin to see the restoration of love, prosperity, wealth and physical wholeness, they will come running, asking, "What must I do to be restored? What must I do to walk in your power?" As the Church of the Lord Jesus Christ, we must begin to walk in our God-given authority! Allow God to restore your soul and you will not walk in lack.

"The Lord is my Shepherd [to feed, guide, and shield me], I shall not lack. He makes me lie down in [fresh, tender] green pastures; He leads me beside the still and restful waters. He refreshes and restores my life (myself)."

—Psalm 23: 1-3 AMP

CHAPTER 4
WEALTH TRANSFERENCE

The Lord gives us numerous examples of wealth transference in His Word. He pointedly said to us in Proverbs 13:22, *"The wealth of the sinner is laid up for the just."* There are other translations of this verse, which says *"Laid up for the righteous is the sinner's wealth." "The wealth of the wicked is treasured up for the righteous." The sinners hoard wealth to pass to the righteous."*

Each translation dictates some form of action taking place between the wicked and the righteous. The wicked has to let go of the wealth and the just have to do something to receive the wealth. It is interesting to note the original Hebrew meaning for the word *"laid"*: *to hoard or reserve; to deny, to protect, hide, keep secretly.*

Literally, this scripture says, the wealth of the wicked has been:
- *hoarded or reserved for the just*
- *denied for the just*
- *protected for the just*
- *hidden for the just*
- *kept secretly for the just*

Hallelujah! Let's take a look at other scriptures which give the connotation of wealth transference:

"This is the portion of a wicked man with God,
and the heritage of oppressors, which they shall
receive of the Almighty. Though he heap up silver
as the dust, and prepare raiment as the clay;
He may prepare it, but the just shall put it on,
and the innocent shall divide the silver."
                                    —Job 27:13, 16, 17

"He who by charging excessive interest and who
by unjust efforts to get gain increases his
material possession gather it for him [to spend]
who is kind and generous to the poor."
                                    —Proverbs 28:8 AMP

"A man to whom God has given riches and
wealth and honor, so that he lacks nothing for
himself of all he desires; yet God does not give
him power to eat of it, but a foreigner consumes it.
This is vanity, and it is an evil affliction."
                                    —Ecclesiastes 6:2 NKJV

"For God giveth to a man that is good in his sight
wisdom, and knowledge, and joy: but to the
sinner he giveth travail, to gather and to heap up,
that he may give to him that is good before
God."
                                    —Ecclesiastes 2:26

God wants to transfer His wealth to His children so we can help finance His Word of Truth. For so long, Satan's disciples have been financing lies—fear, false spirits of drugs, alcoholism, pornography, gambling, etc. Now is the time for God's people to finance and publish the truth of God's Word to a greater degree.

One of the key ways to obtain the transference of wealth is to get before God in prayer to determine what gifts, talents, goods and services you possess or that you could perform for others who are willing to pay you. In our modern day society of hyper-consumption, every time we make a purchase we are transferring wealth to the owner of the goods and services we consume. For example, every time we purchase something from Nike®, we are transferring our wealth to the owner of Nike®. It is time for God's people to dominate and possess wealth by becoming owners and service providers.

THE WEALTH OF THE WICKED

God needs distribution centers to divide and distribute His wealth transference. He is looking for trustworthy believers to share the wealth that will come into the hands of the just. He needs people who can handle money with a mission and do so honestly. God needs good money managers who will be faithful stewards.

Our Heavenly Father will only use those who are unselfish and those who have an understanding that *they are blessed to be a blessing until all the families of the earth are blessed.* (Genesis 12:2) The question is, do you qualify to possess and spread God's wealth?

God wants you blessed because He loves you and He wants you to be able to bless others. God has no problem with you having abundance. In fact, He sent Jesus in the earth so you could have life and have it more abundantly. God has no problem with you being rich, as long as you do not put your trust in those riches.

God confirms this word with the following scriptures:

> "As for the rich in this world, charge them not to
> be proud and arrogant and contemptuous of others,
> nor to set their hopes on uncertain riches, but on
> God, Who richly and ceaselessly provides us with
> everything for [our] enjoyment. [Charge them] to
> do good, to be rich in good works, to be liberal and
> generous of heart, ready to share [with others]."
> —1 Timothy 6:17,18 AMP

The more you give, the more you will receive. When you are rich in good works and willing to share what you have, God richly gives you all things for your enjoyment. I hear many Christians say: "I don't have anything to give; I've already given; I'm tired of being broke, living from paycheck to paycheck. I wish God would be God and do what He promised in His Word."

You must change your mindset. Let us understand, God is not the one holding back the wealth. His provisions have already been made available to you. God's wealth is already here in the earth.
In fact, the earth is full of His riches. What we need to do is determine what are the spiritual roadblocks that are preventing many of us in the Body of Christ from receiving our portion of God's wealth.

When we begin to deal with the multiple root causes which affect our ability to possess God's wealth, we will begin to see more of God's children acquire the wealth God intended for us to have in our possession.

Only through prayer and seeking God will you get an understanding of what is blocking the wealth in store for you. Once you have revelation of what is preventing you from possessing the wealth, begin to make the necessary adjustments in your spirit. Speak the Word of God to those mountains which are preventing you from possessing the wealth.

Your mountain may be getting a revelation that *the blessing of the Lord, it makes rich and He adds no sorrow with it.* (Proverbs 10:22) Maybe it is a lack of creativity and daring to dream big, asking God for witty (clever, creative) inventions.

"I wisdom dwell with prudence, and find out knowledge of witty inventions."
—Proverbs 8:12

For some, it could be a matter of work. God said He would bless the work of your hands. He said the hand of the diligent makes rich. The important question to ask yourself is: "Am I doing the work that God created me and called me to do?"

Perhaps, it may be the words of your mouth and the meditations of your heart that are holding you back. Are your words and your meditations acceptable in God's sight? How about your daily habits— are they pleasing in the eyesight of God?

Locate yourself. Be honest with yourself. Make a decision to change. Come into agreement with God's promises. Begin to spend more time reading God's Word and more time in prayer. Begin saying what God says about His wealth coming into the hands of the just.

We are told in Mark 11:23 that we can have whatsoever we say. By the authority of this scripture we should be confessing that "God's wealth comes to me now!" The Word of God says the wealth that belongs to His children is in the hands of the wicked.

The wealthy wicked are wicked because they have said in their hearts: "my power and the might of my hand have gotten me wealth." (Deuteronomy 8:17) The wealthy wicked fail to recognize and understand that it is God who gave them the power to get the wealth.

Instead, they take full credit for their possessions. They fail to give God the glory that is due to His name. Unless they change from their wicked ways, the earthly possessions they currently have is the only reward they will ever receive.

On the other hand, for the child of God:

 "...it is written, eye has not seen, nor ear heard, neither have entered into the heart of man, the things which God hath prepared for them that love him."
—1 Corinthians 2:9

For us, we have an eternal reward.

Although the Bible refers to wealthy sinners as "wicked," you must understand that God loves the wealthy sinner as much as He loves you and just as much as He loves Jesus. However, God hates their wicked deeds. It is time for those who are just (in right standing with God) to reach out and share the Gospel of Jesus Christ with those who have lost their way.

"God is not willing that any should perish, but that all should come to repentance."
—2 Peter 3:9

Ask your heavenly Father to show you how to win the lost from all lifestyles. Ask the Holy Spirit to teach you how to effectively share the free gift of salvation. I have come to realize that there is no amount of wealth in the earth that can compare with the cost of the shed blood of Jesus our Savior. Jesus paid the ultimate price so that all could have eternal life.

"He that spared not His own Son, but delivered Him up for us all, how shall He not with Him also freely give us all things?"

—Romans 8:32

CHAPTER 5
ARE YOU ELIGIBLE TO RECEIVE THE WEALTH?

The Scripture says the wealth of the sinner is laid up for the just. The just are those who are righteous. This tells me that one must qualify in order to receive God's divine wealth transference. To qualify, you must be in right standing with God.

If you are reading this book and you have never asked Jesus to be Lord of your life, or if you are saved but you are not in right standing with God, you can receive Jesus right now and your fellowship with God can be restored. Put a marker right here and go to page 188 and follow the instructions. Your life will never be the same. Hallelujah!

> "Giving thanks to the Father, Who has qualified
> and made us fit to share in the portion which is the
> inheritance of the saints (God's holy people) in
> the Light."
>
> —Colossians 1:12 AMP

In other words, God has:

> *...Made you sufficient*
> *...Entitled you*
> *...Fitted you*
> *...Qualified you*

You qualify to share in the portion of the wealth which awaits God's people. The people of God are those living in the Light —Jesus, the Light of the world. If you are a born again believer, that is, if you have confessed Jesus as Lord of your life, you believe the Word of God and you are living according to God's Word, you qualify to receive the sinner's wealth! So why haven't you possessed the wealth?

Could it be that you are not firmly persuaded that God will do what He said He would do? God is waiting on you to come into agreement with His Word. Don't you know? Haven't you heard? We have the Spirit of the Lord living on the inside of us and where the Spirit of the Lord is there is liberty!

Yes! We have freedom to possess the promised blessings! We are **FREE** to **DOMINATE** wealth here in the earth. With this freedom, it is time to move from the promise to the possession.

While conducting a personal finance seminar recently, I asked the following question: "How many of you could see yourself as a millionaire?" Very few hands went up. One person responded by saying that she could not see herself having that much money. There are many believers with the same mindset. This kind of thought process does not line up or agree with our God of Abundance, *El Shaddai*. He is our all-sufficient God who has more than enough to give us an abundant supply.

God is a God of increase and He wants to increase you more and more, you and your children. (Psalm 115:14) He wants to put wealth and riches in your house! (Psalm 112:1-3) We must allow God to be God! It is time to put on the mind of Christ and begin to think like Jesus did.

The mind of Christ has no boundaries. The mind of Christ knows that there are no impossibilities with God because God is a Big God. I challenge you to begin to think the way God thinks. Think big! If you think you can, you will. If you think you cannot, you will not. Whatever you think and believe in your heart, you eventually become. Where you are today is a direct result of what you imagined and then spoke into existence.

I challenge you today to begin seeing yourself as a wealthy person. Meditate on what it would be like if you had a perfect day. Take time to dream about the life God created you to live. If you can see it by faith, you can receive it. Begin to see yourself as more than a conqueror. Picture yourself as an overcomer, knowing that you *can* do all things through Christ which strengthens you. (Philippians 4:13)

When obstacles of lack and financial deficiencies get in your way, overcome them! The Word of God tells us that we overcome the enemy by the blood of the Lamb and by the word of our testimony. (Revelation 12:11) The blood of the Lamb was shed over 2000 years ago when Jesus was crucified on the cross for you and I. That part of overcoming was taken care of for you.

Now it's time to do your part. You must learn how to appropriate the blood, pleading it against sickness, poverty and lack. Applying the power of the blood of Jesus to negative situations will bring victory. Next, you need to share the word of your testimony. Tell of God's goodness and what He has done in your life so that you, and those hearing your testimony, can have hope to overcome!

Ask God to give you the power (His ability) to get wealth. Take time to listen for His directions, then do what He tells you to do. You will find yourself having an awesome testimony of how God provided increase in your life.

Wouldn't you like to testify that no man has made you rich but the Lord? Through the shed blood of Jesus Christ, we have access to God's Throne. We have access to all God owns. He owns the earth, the fullness thereof, and all that dwells in the earth. He owns it and we have access to partake of all that He owns.

Anytime you run into lack, testify that —

> "The Lord is my Shepherd; I shall not want."
> —Psalm 23:1

Speak to the negative situations in your life. Say it is written:

> "…No good thing will He withhold from me
> because I walk uprightly."
> —Psalm 84:11

Find scriptures that promise you the things you need from God. Speak those promises and testify that it shall be done in Jesus' Name! God's Word is true and God is faithful. He can be counted on to do what He said He would do.

Do not allow these obstacles listed below to keep you from possessing your Heavenly Father's wealth. Stop living in guilt, fear and in bondage. Get free today!

Free From What People Think
Free From Fear of Having Too Much
Free From Inferiority---You Are Good Enough to be Wealthy
Free From Condemnation

You are a child of God, led by His Spirit; therefore, there is no condemnation to your being wealthy. Forget about what people think. Your acquisition of wealth is to establish God's covenant promises here in the earth. Your attainment and preservation of wealth is for God's mission here in the earth.

> "But thou shalt remember the Lord thy God:
> for it is He that giveth thee power to get wealth,
> that He may establish His covenant which He
> sware unto thy fathers, as it is this day."
> —Deuteronomy 8:18

CHAPTER 6
BORN TO BE WEALTHY

O ne day as I sat watching the movie *The Lion King*®, the Lord ministered to me by showing me in His Word that *"The righteous are bold as a lion."* (Proverbs 28:1) The lion, as we know, is often referred to as the "king of the jungle."

As children of God, we are peculiar people from a royal priesthood. We are kings in the earth. Jesus said He is the King of Kings. Scripture further tells us that Jesus is the *Prince of the kings in the earth.* (Revelation 1:5) Imagine. God sees you as a great king here in the earth. Two of the attributes of a king are that kings reign and rule. Whatever kings decree must come to pass. That is exciting!

> "You shall decree a thing and it shall be established!"
> —Job 22:28

I challenge you to become who God said you are. Christians are not supposed to be passive.

> "The kingdom of heaven suffereth violence, and the violent take it by force."
> —Matthew 11:12

The force is in the power of God's Word. His Word is powerful, active, operative and on the move to perform that which He said it would do. If we are going to possess the wealth God has in store, we must take it by force. Put the Word of God in your mouth and confess:

> *Father, in the Name of Jesus, I believe in my heart and say with my mouth that Your Word has power, and Your Word rules over every area in my life. Thank You for empowering me to be Your child. (John 1:12) Thank You for empowering me to get wealth. (Deuteronomy 8:18) Because I walk uprightly before You, no good thing will You withhold from me. (Psalm 84:11) You promised to give me good and perfect things because every good gift comes from You, my Father of lights. (James 1:17)*

> *I am asking You for wisdom to obtain the wealth which You have stored up for me. Show me how to possess it, share it, and preserve it for the end time harvesting of souls.*

> *Because I am a giver, I declare gifts will be multiplied back to me. (Luke 6:38) Right now, You are increasing me more and more, me and my children. (Psalm 115:14) You are multiplying me a thousand times by blessing me as you promised. (Deuteronomy 1:11) You are causing me to live the abundant life—a God kind of life that is super-abundant in quantity and superior in quality. (John 10:10)*

> *Lord, You are my Shepherd; therefore, I shall not want. Thank You for restoring to me sevenfold of everything the thief has stolen. (Proverbs 6:31) Thank You for making all grace, every favor and earthly blessing come to me in abundance, that I am always, under all circumstances, and whatever the need, totally self-sufficient. I have enough to require no aid or support, and I am furnished in abundance*

for every good work and charitable donation.
(2 Corinthians 9:8 Amp)

Because I am a good man/woman, I will leave an inheritance
for my children's children. This is an inheritance of godly
living with a pure heart and a legacy of wealth. In the
authority of Jesus, I believe I receive and I release my faith
and call these things done! Hallelujah!

Having done all to stand, stand. Continue believing, trusting, praising and worshipping God. Continue to confess God's promises and continue to expect the manifestation of God's ability to perform His Word until you possess the wealth! Then thank, praise and worship Him forever more!

> "Let them praise the name of the Lord: for His name
> alone is excellent; His glory is above the earth and
> heaven."
>   —Psalm 148:13

The RESPONSIBILITY Is Yours!

GOD SAID:

He takes pleasure in your prosperity. (Psalm 35:27)

Wealth and riches shall be in your house. (Psalm 112:3)

No good thing will He withhold from you. (Psalm 84:11)

He freely gives us all things. (Romans 8:32)

For your sake Jesus became poor, that you through
His poverty might be rich. (2 Corinthians 8:9)

You shall be abundantly satisfied with the fatness of
His house; and He will make you drink of the river of
His pleasures. (Psalm 36:8)

He provides you with peace, prosperity, security, and
stability. (Jeremiah 33:9)

Be joyful in the day of prosperity. (Ecclesiastes 7:14)

Peace and prosperity shall be within your walls.
(Psalm 122:7)

YOU Have The RIGHT!

GOD SAID:

"But as many as received Him, to them gave He the
power to become the sons of God, even to them that
 believe on His name."
                                        —John 1:12

"For as many as are led by the Spirit of God they are the
sons of God. And if children, then heirs; heirs of God,
and joint-heirs with Christ."
                                        —Romans 8:14, 17

"The earth is the Lord's, and the fullness thereof; the world,
and they that dwell therein."
                                        —Psalm 24:1

"The silver is mine, and the gold is mine, saith the Lord
of hosts."
                                        —Haggai 2:8

The Israelites (God's children), in the Old Testament, exercised their right and fulfilled their responsibility in possessing the sinner's wealth. Let us look at a profound example of the wealth of the sinner being transferred to the just.

When the Israelites were in bondage in Egypt, they cried out to their God. God heard their cry and delivered them out of bondage. Are you in the bondage of debt today? Are you in the bondage of having just enough or not having enough? Cry out to God. He said,

> "His eyes are on the righteous and His ears are open
> to their cry."
> —Psalm 34:15

God instructed the women of Israel to go to their neighbors and borrow silver, gold, and fine linen so that when they came out of bondage, they wouldn't come out empty. (Exodus 3:21, 22) Praise the Lord! Just as God gave the Israelites favor with their oppressor, He will grant you favor to possess the wealth that's been hidden for you. He is the same yesterday, today and forever. He is the Lord your God who changes not.

There were two levels of wealth transference which took place when God's children came out of bondage. First, the Egyptians (those who had God's people in bondage) gave the wealth to the women of Israel when they asked for it. Oh! What an awesome miracle!
Secondly, the women of Israel gave wealth to their offspring. God does not intend for you to hoard the wealth once you gain possession of it. You must distribute the wealth according to God's instructions.

Proverbs 13:22 reminds us, *"A good man leaveth an inheritance for his children's children: and the wealth of the sinner is laid up for the just."* There is a connector to possessing the wealth. Sharing is the connector. God intends for you to share the wealth you possess. God said that He will bless you to be a blessing until all the families of the earth are blessed. (Genesis 12:3) Never forget that you are blessed to be a blessing.

Before the wealth was given to the Israelites, God gave specific instructions, and the women in turn, obeyed those instructions. What has God instructed you to do? Are you doing it? Imagine what would have happened if the women decided they did not "feel" like going to their neighbor to ask for the wealth?

God would not have brought them out also with silver and gold. (Psalm 105:37) They probably would not have been filled with joy and gladness, but they would have remained broke and in bondage.

> "...To obey is better than sacrifice..."
> —1 Samuel 15:22

CHAPTER 7
OBEDIENCE IS THE KEY

One of the essential factors in possessing the wealth that is stored up for you is your obedience. The Lord reminds us in Isaiah 1:19 that: If you be willing and obedient, you shall eat the good of the land. The "good" of the land means the best of the land. As I mentioned in my introduction, it is God's desire that you have the good of the land.

God desires that you drive the best, live in the best, wear the best, and become the best He created you to be. To attain the best, you must be willing AND obedient. One without the other will not yield God's best.

Understand that everything God intends for you and I to enjoy in this time was made possible at the cross through the shed blood of Jesus of Nazareth. It is up to us to possess the blessings in store for us. We must be obedient and take action by doing whatever God instructs us to do in order to possess the wealth.

Before Jesus performed His first miracle, His mother gave specific instructions to the servants. Her instructions were, "Whatever He says to you, do it." In order for Jesus to perform the miracle, the servants had to participate with Him.

Jesus gave specific instructions, i.e., fill the water pots with water. Take some out and give it to the manager of the feast. When the manager of the feast tasted the water, at that point the water turned into wine! (See John 2:9) We can see that, in order for Jesus to perform the miracle, His servants had to do what they were told to do. The servants had to take action and participate in their miracle.

In order for you to possess the wealth, you have to act upon God's instructions. You will need to take action. For example, He may tell you to leave one job and do something else which makes no sense to you. The Lord may instruct you to do something that's outside of your comfort zone.

Perhaps the Lord may tell you to purchase a piece of property in an undesirable location. What you don't know is that within 12 months a new development in the neighboring area will be underway which will increase the value of your property 1,000 times. There have been true accounts of this happening. God has millions of ways of empowering you to possess the wealth.

Many people rationalize themselves out of their miracle because their head gets in the way. It's time to lose your mind and get the mind of Christ. The Bible tells us to—

> "Let this mind be in you, which was also in Christ Jesus."
> —Philippians 2:5

Jesus was selfless. He always did the will of His Father.

The mind that was also in Christ Jesus, in the form of being obedient unto death, has enabled Him to create wealth and an inheritance for our heavenly Father. Today, God continues to be made rich through the harvest of souls stemming from Jesus' obedience to stay on the cross unto death. Great rewards come from being obedient to God!

Follow God's instructions. Do what He tells you to do, when He tells you to do it. God has an expected end for your life. God has a divine plan and purpose for your life. He created you and He knows what you are supposed to do every second of your life. Therefore, it is imperative that you listen to His instructions. His thoughts are higher than your thoughts. His ways are higher than your ways. (Isaiah 55:9) Hear God's thoughts and go His way. When the Spirit of the Lord speaks to you, do what He says! You may ask the question, "How will I know if God is speaking?"

When God Speaks: You will have a knowing that you know it's the right thing to do. You will have peace. Always let peace by your umpire. God will gently guide you. He will never force you to do anything. You will not feel rushed. You will not be confused. You will have clarity. You will receive confirmation that this is the right thing to do. Lastly, God's instructions will be in agreement with His Word.

When you think God is speaking but it's actually you: There will be questioning versus knowing. There will be hesitation, deception, lack of clarity, double- mindedness, and desires that are not godly.

When the enemy speaks: You will have fear, doubt, discomfort, conflict, restlessness, wonderment (is this really God?), confusion, guilt, and discouragement. This voice does not agree with God's Word. (See 1 John 4:1-3) This voice comes with deception and there is no truth in what the enemy says. He is a liar and the father of lies. (John 8:44)

Begin to train your spirit to hear that still, small voice (The Holy Spirit) as you spend time in prayer. Follow His leading and do according to His instructions. Allow me to share, from my own life, an example of hearing and obeying the voice of the Lord.

Earlier I mentioned that we overcome the enemy by the blood of the Lamb and the word of our testimony. It is time for me to testify. In the spring of 2000, I was impressed by an inward knowing to leave an illustrious 14-year banking career to go into full-time ministry. When I announced that I was leaving my banking career, many thought I was crazy.

I must admit this was a big risk. I was giving up a great job that I really enjoyed most of the time; a job where I had tremendous favor, respect, a comfortable salary, and excellent benefits. However, I knew in my heart that preaching the gospel was my divine call and this was the set time to step out and trust God. This was truly a big walk of faith.

One day, as I was fasting and praying during lunchtime, I was led to a scripture found in Mark 10:28-30. In summary, the scripture says, "there is no man that has given up and left house or brothers or sisters or mother or father or children or lands for My sake and the Gospel's who will not receive a hundred times as much now in this time, houses and brothers and sisters and mothers and children and lands, with persecutions."

The Word of God assured me that whatever I give up for God's sake and the Gospel's sake, I would receive a hundred fold in this time. Oh! Don't forget, with persecutions. Prior to submitting my resignation letter, I received some devastating, life shattering news— the type of news that would make you want to give up on life and crawl into a hole.

Although the news was devastating, I had a word of promise from God. One word from God can strengthen you and encourage you to go on. Through faith, I gave my three-week resignation and I left my good-paying corporate job as a Vice President of a major bank.

I resigned from the bank on May 17, 2000. On that same day, I went into full-time ministry. Immediately, persecution came. A few weeks later, one of our fully paid, late model cars was totaled in an accident. We had just purchased several cans of paint, which were on the back seat of the car. Someone ran into our parked car, and the paint spilled onto the entire interior of the car, totaling the car.

Shortly thereafter, we painted and remodeled our kitchen and purchased three new bedroom suites. December 31st of that same year, while we were in New Years Eve service, we lost the contents of our home to a devastating fire. Yes, we lost the new furniture, the newly remodeled kitchen and all the gifts, as we had just celebrated Christmas. All we had in the natural were the clothes on our backs and the shoes on our feet.

My pastor had declared in that New Years Eve service that 2001 would be a year of restoration. I grabbed onto that word and that promise. I can tell you that God is performing His Word; since that time, my family and I have increased in every area of our lives. Our tithes and offerings doubled. We became debt free with the exception of our mortgage. We also received two late model luxury cars, paid in full. We lost our house, but our home remained intact. We got full revelation that a house is not a home. Our lives had been spared and that was enough to thank God for.

The restoration process continued. God blessed us with a miracle house—a new, larger, newly furnished house. Deuteronomy 6:11 was fulfilled in our lives. God gave us a house full of all good things, which we did not pay for. Hallelujah! God pays for whatever He orders!

We lost all of our clothing; however, we now have a new wardrobe for our family of four. We have also obtained financial miracles upon miracles and our marriage and family are stronger in the Lord. Glory to God!

When I was making the decision to follow God's instructions about leaving the bank, I was "believing" God for a new house. One of the questions the enemy kept asking me was, "How are you going to get a new house with one pay stub?" In other words, "how will you qualify for a mortgage with only one income?"

Well, thank God, Who always cause us to triumph! We have a new house and we didn't have to show proof of income because God qualified us and gave it to us free! *God is able to do exceeding abundantly above all we ask or think!* (Ephesians 3:20)

Wait! There is more! The good news is that our eyes haven't seen nor our ears heard the wonderful things God has prepared for us! Praise the Lord, there is more in store! Yes—persecution will come; afflictions will come. But the Lord will deliver you out of them all (Psalm 34:19). What the enemy meant for harm, God turned it into good.

I believe God honored my obedience and the faith to trust Him to be my abundant supply. For God, it's never an issue of money; it's always an issue of, "where is your faith?" I was willing to give up a sizeable income for the Gospel's sake. I knew in my heart that He would provide because He is the God of pre-vision and provision. Again, God pays for what He orders. He has done just that and more.

The Bible reminds us in Proverbs 13:22 AMP, *"The wealth of the sinner [find its way eventually] into the hands of the righteous, for whom it was laid up."* Many people quote this pivotal scripture without having full revelation of what it truly means.

If those who are just (in right standing with God) had full revelation of what God meant when He said "the wealth of the sinner is laid up for the just," the just would be acquiring that wealth and bringing it into their possession. The Israelites had to **DO SOMETHING** to possess the wealth, and so do you!

Again, I ask: What has God told you to do? Are you doing it? On the other side of your obedience, there is wealth and increase. Your blessings from God are waiting on your obedience to God. The Lord said,

> " If you are willing and obedient, you shall eat the good of the land."
>
> —Isaiah 1:19

Your willingness to adhere to and do God's Word will bring success. Partial obedience is disobedience. In other words, one could be obedient to do what God said to do, yet not have a willing heart while doing it.

> "If they OBEY and serve Him, they shall spend their days in prosperity, and their years in pleasure."
>
> —Job 36:11
> (emphasis added)

CHAPTER 8
BLESSINGS OF OBEDIENCE

In Deuteronomy Chapter 28, verses one through 14 (AMP), the Word of God outlines the blessings of being obedient to God's voice. God's voice is His Word. *"If you will listen diligently to the voice of the Lord your God, being watchful to do all His commandments which I command you this day,"* the Lord your God said:

> *He will set you high above all the nations of the earth.*

> *Blessings shall come upon you and overtake you.*

> *Blessed shall you be in the city and blessed shall you be in the field—wherever you go, you will be blessed.*

> *Blessed shall you be in the fruit of your body and the fruit of your ground and the fruit of your beasts, the increase of your cattle and the young of your flock—you, your kids, your finances and your belongings will be blessed.*

> *Blessed shall be your basket and your store—you will be blessed financially.*

*Blessed shall you be when you come in and blessed shall
you be when you go out.*

*The Lord shall cause your enemies who rise up against
you to be defeated before your face: they shall come out
against you one way and flee before you seven ways.*

*The Lord shall command the blessing upon you in your
storehouse and in all that you undertake. And He will
bless you in the land which the Lord your God gives you.*

*The Lord will establish you as a people holy to Himself,
as He has sworn to you, if you keep the commandments of
the Lord your God and walk in His ways.*

*And all the people of the earth shall see that you are called
by the name [and in the presence of] the Lord, and they
shall be afraid of you.*

…The Lord shall make you have a surplus of prosperity.

*The Lord shall open to you His good treasury, the heavens,
to give the rain of your land in its season and to bless all
the work of your hands;*

…You shall lend to many nations but you shall not borrow.

…The Lord shall make you the head and not the tail.

*…You shall be above only, and you shall not be beneath,
if you heed the commandments of the Lord your God which
I command you this day and are watchful to do them.*

It is God's desire to bless you abundantly by empowering you to
prosper! God wants you to prosper spiritually, physically, and

financially. Although these covenant promises belong to you, in order to receive them, you must do your part. These covenant blessings are between you and God.

This is a two-sided deal. In fact, when you do not do your part, you will get the opposite of the promised blessings. If you continue reading the remainder of Deuteronomy chapter 28, you will see what happens when you choose not to do things God's way.

The promises of God are conditional "if - then" promises. If you do your part (obey His voice and do what His Word tells you to do), then God will do His part. God will ensure His blessings will overtake you. It is that simple. Whether or not you receive these promises is contingent upon whether or not you are keeping your part of the deal.

The first thing God said before He spoke about the outpouring of blessings was: "if you diligently listen to My voice." How do you hear His voice? By hearing and hearing His Word. By reading His Word and by meditating on His Word. The Bible is God's voice speaking to you.

The second instruction was, "if you are watchful to do what My Word says to do, then, all the aforementioned blessings shall overtake you." You will never receive a full measure of God's blessings and provisions unless you grow up in Him by reading, studying, and meditating upon His Word, and doing what His Word says to do.

God made precious promises in His Word. He is a Promise Keeper. All of His promises are Yes and Amen—so be it (2 Corinthians 1:20). The rest is up to you. We must agree with God's Word and participate with God by doing His Word. God will do what He said He would do.

"God is not a man, that he should tell or act a lie; neither the son of man, that he should feel repentance or compunction [For what He has promised]. Has He said and shall he not do it? Or has He spoken and shall he not make it good?"

—Numbers 23:19 AMP

CHAPTER 9
WHAT IS WEALTH?

According to Noah Webster's **1828 American Dictionary of The English Language**, the definition of *"wealth"* is:

Prosperity—advance or gain in anything good or desirable; successful progress in any business or enterprise; success; attainment of object desired;

Riches; large possessions of money, goods or land

Affluence; opulence; external happiness

Some would term the following statement as a common sense definition of wealth: Having possessions which produces a surplus of income to such an extent that a return on your possessions will enable you to live in luxury or in the manner you desire without having to work next week, next year, or many years to come if you choose to do so. Wealth produced from these possessions would support your children and grandchildren for many generations.

According to **Webster's New Riverside Dictionary**, a *"wealthy person"* is one *having much wealth; one who is affluent; richly supplied; and one who has abundance.* This description is fit for a child of God, is it not?

We have affluence because God created us in His image. We know that God is all-powerful. He is a King and He reigns. God is a God of wealth, affluence, splendor and majesty. When you received Jesus as Lord and Savior, you automatically gained the privilege of becoming a child of God. With the attributes of God comes the privilege of being heirs of God.

Remember, as children of God, we are of a royal priesthood. We are in a kingly state of being. We are richly supplied, because God said, "He richly supplies us with all things to enjoy." Furthermore, we have abundance because Jesus said, "He came so we could have life and life more abundantly." (1 Timothy 6:17; John 10:10) It bears repeating that the abundant life is the God kind of life—a good life that is superior in quality and abundant in quantity. Yes! God sent Jesus for you to have an exceptional life. Yes! You and I were created to be wealthy!

The word *"wealthy"* is mentioned two times in the Bible: Psalm 66:12 *"…But thou brought us out into a wealthy place."* This word *"wealthy"* in the original Hebrew text means *"wealth that runs over."* That sounds like the overflow to me! God wants to bring His children to a place of overflow where His blessings upon us run over. Hallelujah!

The second place in the Bible where *"wealthy"* is mentioned is found in Jeremiah 49:31, which says: *"Arise get you up unto the wealthy nation, that dwelleth without care, saith the Lord, which have neither gates nor bars, which dwell alone."*

There is a place of wealth reserved for God's people; however, it is up to us to get up to that wealthy place. We get there through faith and trust in God and His Word. Find scriptures that promise you your wealth, then allow those scriptures to become one with you, engrafted in you until your mind, will and emotions agree with and become settled in the truth that God wants you wealthy.

Meditate on the fact that God's Word is truth. His Word is settled in heaven. (John 17:17; Psalm 119:89) Meditate on what God says about blessing you until you believe and expect to be in your wealthy place.

When some people think of wealth, their thought process is limited to financial wealth. However, wealth has other forms. There is also spiritual, physical, as well as personal financial wealth. In fact, to be truly wealthy is to be full of love, joy, peace, longsuffering, kindness, goodness, faithfulness, gentleness, and self-control, all of which money cannot buy. (See Galatians 5:22)

In the original Hebrew text, the word *"wealth"* means being *at ease, peaceable, prosper, prosperity, quietness, and wealthy.* God wants you to get to the place where you live in financial overflow as well as physical and spiritual overflow. He wants you to possess the wealth and live a quiet, peaceable, prosperous life with ease where nothing is missing or broken—spiritually, physically or financially. That's true wealth!

The word *"wealth"* is mentioned 27 times in the King James Version of the Bible. I will bring to light a few of these scriptures along with the original Hebrew meaning of the word *"wealth"* which has been denoted within the brackets.

> "To whom God has given riches, wealth [to accumulate treasures, riches, and wealth]."
> —Ecclesiastes 6:19

> "I rejoiced because my wealth [power, riches, strength] was great."
> —Job 31:35

"That God gives thee the power to get wealth [great forces of goods, power, riches, strength]."
—Deuteronomy 8:18

" They spend their days in wealth [prosperity, pleasure, joyful]."
—Job 21:13

"Wealth [riches, substance, wealth] of the wicked is laid up for the just."
—Proverbs 13:22

The wealth we are to possess from the wicked will bring us joy, pleasure and prosperity. That is why the Lord says in Psalm 35:27: *"Let them shout for joy, and be glad, that favor my righteous cause: yea, let them say continually, Let the Lord be magnified, which hath pleasure in the prosperity of His servant."*

We have an obligation to bring pleasure to our Lord. When we favor His righteous cause (His Word and His way of doing things) we will prosper spiritually, physically and financially. Then, our Lord will be magnified.

"Oh, magnify the Lord with me, and let us exalt His name together! "
—Psalm 43:3

Go and possess the wealth!

CHAPTER 10

WHO HAS THE WEALTH?

According to the 2003 Forbes financial report, the top 10 wealthiest Americans were either business owners, founders of business or business executives of profitable companies.[1] In short, the origin of their wealth stemmed from some form of business.

According to a recent Internal Revenue Service article titled *"Personal Wealth,"* the analysis of wealth in America shows Americans were enjoying the greatest level of prosperity than ever before. Then the economic downturn began late in the year 2000, where many Americans lost their life savings due to sluggish market conditions and corporate scandals. That is why I caution you not to put your trust in riches—they grow wings and fly away. (Proverbs 23:5) It is far better to put your trust in God.

The Internal Revenue Service article went on to say that there is approximately $15 trillion dollars in accumulated wealth in the United States. There are currently 270 million Americans, which represent approximately 150 million households. Ten percent of these households own 90 percent of the $15 trillion in personal wealth.

These statistics are both staggering and disappointing. It is apparent from these statistics that a small percentage of the people own most of the wealth. Do you wonder what the wealthy 10 percent are doing that the other 90 percent are not doing? I believe the wealthy 10 percent have attained wisdom and understanding on how to accumulate and preserve wealth.

The book of Proverbs is very clear about the end results of chasing fantasies—this leads to poverty. However, the person who works will have plenty of bread (Proverbs 28:19). Many Christians have a desire to be wealthy; however, few achieve financial success, namely because they are following worthless pursuits, having no understanding of their purpose and the call (a divine invitation to do something specific) of God on their lives.

Many believers also fail to take the time to learn how to become financially successful. It is almost as though we are waiting for wealth and riches to fall from the sky, when the reality is God's provisions are already here in the earth. We are not waiting on God; He is waiting on us to possess His wealth and His true riches.

The individuals who achieve financial success and become wealthy are those who:

- **Seek godly counsel**, although many do not recognize that it is the wisdom of God which causes them to be wealthy. Keep in mind, God is so good that He rains on the just and the unjust (Matthew 5:45).

- **Understand the nature and scope of money**

- **Utilize their God-given talents**

- **Ask for and utilize creativity**

- Are able to imagine or visualize themselves being wealthy

- Have developed good work habits

- Understand time is money and therefore do not waste time

- Understand that the borrower is a slave to the lender

- Have an attitude of wealth

- Are disciplined in their saving and spending habits

- Don't have to have everything now and therefore exercise delayed gratification

- Take the time to become knowledgeable about financial matters

- Know how to live beneath their means

- Ensure their income is greater than their monthly expenses

"O Lord, how manifold are thy works! In wisdom
hast thou made them all; the earth is full of thy riches."
—Psalm 104:24

WISDOM + UNDERSTANDING = WEALTH

The world in which we live today is wealthy namely because of the
wisdom and knowledge God has put in the earth. The earth is full of

God's knowledge and His wisdom and therefore the earth is full of God's wealth. God has given mankind His ability to do all things. All of the wealth God intends for His children to possess is already in the earth. Are you surprised? I believe some people think God is going to part the heavens and throw cars, houses, and bags of money into the hands of His children. No! That is not going to happen!

Instead, He said He will empower you to get wealth. (Deuteronomy 8:18) Here God is saying He will anoint you to prosper. He will give you His ability and His efficiency to prosper. He further said He would teach you how to profit, instruct you, and teach you the way in which you should go (Isaiah 48:17). God said He would guide you with His eye (His intellect, His knowledge). (Psalm 32:8)

When we allow God to guide by His intellect and knowledge, He will lead us to our wealthy place. The primary reason believers do not have the wealth is because we do not fully rely on the leading of the Holy Spirit. Another reason we have not amassed wealth is because we do not have the knowledge and God's wisdom of how to possess the wealth. Oh! That has to change!

We must begin to walk in the light of the Word. God's Word is the lamp unto our feet, and the light to our pathway to possessing the wealth. (Psalm 119:105) When we follow God's Word, we are bound to become wise and possess the wealth. The wealth in the earth has been "heaped up" and preserved for us. Get wisdom. Get wealth.

> "For God gives to a man that is good in his sight:
> wisdom, and knowledge, and joy: but to the sinner
> he gives travail, to gather and to heap up, that he may
> give to him that is good before God."
> —Ecclesiastes 2:26

Recently I was driving across the Chesapeake Bay Bridge, a massive bridge built over water near Annapolis, Maryland. This was one of the most magnificent experiences I have ever had. This bridge is one of the world's longest and most scenic over-water structures, which spans 4.3 miles shore to shore. As I drove across the bridge, I was in total awe of the wisdom God gave man to architect and construct such a massive masterpiece. Without a doubt, the owners of the architectural and construction firms gained tremendous wealth from following God's intellect and His knowledge.

It is this kind of wisdom that made the biblical character Solomon the wealthiest man that ever lived. He built the beautiful Solomon's Temple. If it were in existence today, some say the temple would be worth over $550 billion dollars. What did Solomon possess that allowed him to garner this wealth? Solomon had Wisdom and an Understanding heart given to him by a loving God. The Lord appeared to Solomon in a dream and asked what he would like to receive of God. Solomon's response was:

> "Give thy servant an understanding heart." And God said unto him, because thou hast asked this thing, and hast not asked for thyself long life; neither hast asked riches for thyself, nor hast asked the life of your enemies: but hast asked for thyself understanding to discern judgment; Behold, I have done according to thy words: lo, I have given thee a WISE and UNDERSTANDING heart. And I have also given thee that which thou hast not asked both RICHES, and HONOUR."
> —1 Kings 3:9, 11-13
> (emphasis added)

SOLOMON'S GOD BRINGS HIM WEALTH

When the queen of Sheba heard of the fame (the wealth and wisdom) of Solomon, she came to see him and brought with her great wealth of camels, spices, much gold, and precious stones.

> "When the queen of Sheba heard of [the constant connection of] the fame of Solomon with the name of the Lord, she came to prove him with hard questions (problems and riddles)."
>
> —1 King 10:1 AMP

> "And when the queen of Sheba had seen all Solomon's wisdom, and the house that he had built, and the meat of his table, and the sitting of his servants, and the attendance of his ministers, and their apparel, and his cupbearers, and his ascent by which he went up unto the house of the Lord; there was no more spirit in her. And she said to the king, it was a true report that I heard in mine own land of thy acts and of thy wisdom. Howbeit I believed not the words, until I came, and mine eyes had SEEN it; and behold, the half was not told me; thy wisdom and prosperity exceeds the fame which I heard."
>
> —1 Kings 10:4-7

The queen fainted when she saw Solomon's wealth and when she saw how Solomon reverenced his God. Remember, she heard that Solomon's wealth was connected to the name of the Lord. The story goes on to say that the queen gave Solomon an abundance of gold, spices and precious stones. (1 King 10:10 AMP)

> "Now the weight of the gold that came to Solomon in one [particular] year was 666 talents of gold."
>
> —1 Kings 10:14 AMP

Six hundred and sixty six talents would be worth about $19.5 million dollars today!

How do you like that? This was wealth transference. Solomon's wisdom attracted the wealth of the wicked and he possessed their wealth. When the people SAW his PROSPERITY and SAW his WISDOM, they came to him in droves.

Solomon was able to minister to those who were without God and they began to serve the God he served. God will empower you to prosper so that you can be a witness to the lost.

> "He that wins souls is wise."
> —Proverbs 11:30

Seek the Lord with all your heart. In all your ways acknowledge Him and He will direct your path. (Proverbs 3:5)

Ask Him for wisdom and power to possess the wealth. He will empower you with God ideas. Get wisdom and get an understanding on how to get the wealth! Hallelujah!

> "I wisdom dwell with prudence, and find out knowledge of witty inventions."
> —Proverbs 8:12

CHAPTER 11
WEALTH-BUILDING SCRIPTURES

T he Word of God tells us that *faith comes by hearing and hearing by the Word of God.* (Romans 10:17) In order for you to possess the wealth which is in store, you must have faith in God. Everything we receive from God is through faith. You must be firmly persuaded that God truly wants you to possess the wealth He has created for you.

It is also important that you develop a spirit of faith to believe God when He said He will give you power (His ability) to get wealth. What is the spirit of faith? It is simply believing God's written promises to the point where you have no doubt that the promise is for you, and then speaking what you believe.

> "We having the same spirit of faith, according as
> it is written, I believed, and therefore have I spoken;
> we also believe, and therefore speak."
> —2 Corinthians 4:13

Everything God does is by His Spirit.

> "Not by might, nor by power, but by My Spirit says the
> Lord."
> —Zechariah 4:6

Everything done "God's way" begins in the Spirit. Know that the Spirit of the Lord does nothing without His Word.

In order for you to speak and see the promise come to pass, you must use God's Word. God upholds all things by His mighty Word of power. (Hebrews 1:3) God hastens to perform His Word so that no word from Him is void of power, but it shall accomplish that which He pleases, and it shall prosper in the thing whereto He sends it. (Jeremiah 1:12, Isaiah 55:11)

There is power to create wealth in your mouth and in your heart. Get the Word of God down deep in your heart, because what you create with your mouth is what's in your heart. (Matthew 15:18)

> "Out of the abundance of the heart, the mouth speaks."
> —Matthew 12:34

We make wealth deposits by putting God's Word in our heart and then speaking the goodness of God's Word out of our mouths. God said,

> "I create the fruit of the lips."
> —Isaiah 57:19

Fruit is produce. God will produce His words, which come from your lips.

It's time to take back what the devil stole from you! Enough is enough! You do not have to put up with the pressure of lack. You do not have to live in mediocrity. You can live in superiority!

The following are *"wealth-building"* scriptures to help you build your faith to receive the wealth. Meditate on these scriptures. Believe God's Word in your heart and begin to speak them daily.

Abram had become very wealthy in livestock and in silver and gold. (Genesis 13:2 NIV) We are Abraham's seed and God promised to bless the seed of Abraham. (See Galatians 3:13, 14, 29 NIV) Put your name in these scriptures and begin to call yourself wealthy.

> "The man became rich, and his wealth continued to grow until he became very wealthy."
>
> —Genesis 26:13 NIV

> "Surely all the wealth that God took away from our father belongs to us and our children, so do whatever God has told you."
>
> —Genesis 31:16 NIV

> "You may say to yourself, "My power and the strength of my hands have produced this wealth for me." But remember the Lord your God, for it is he who gives you the ability to produce wealth, and so confirms his covenant, which he swore to your forefathers, as it is today."
>
> —Deuteronomy 8:17, 18 NIV

> "Wealth and honor come from you (God); you are the ruler of all things. In your hands are strength and power to exalt and give strength to all."
>
> —1 Chronicles 29:12 NIV

> "Do you not know from of old, since the time that man was placed on the earth, that the triumphing of the wicked is short, and the joy of the godless and defiled is but for a moment?"
>
> —Job 20: 4-5 AMP

"His (the enemy, the wicked) children must make amends
to the poor; his own hands must give back his wealth."
—Job 20:10 NIV

"...his hands will give back his [ill-gotten] wealth."
—Job 20:14 AMP

"Do not steal, cheat or lie to one another. Do not cheat
or rob anyone. Be sure to pay hired workers promptly."
—Leviticus 19:11

"Because I put my trust in the Lord, I shall be
abundantly satisfied with the fatness of His house
and God makes me drink of the river of His pleasure."
—Psalm 36:8

"Be not afraid when (an ungodly) one is made rich,
when the wealth and glory of his house are increased;
for when he dies he will carry nothing away; his glory
will not descend after him. "
—Psalm 49:16-17

"Here now is the man who did not make God his
stronghold but trusted in his great wealth and grew
strong by destroying others. Surely God will bring you
down to everlasting ruin: He will snatch you up and
tear you from your tent; He will uproot you from the
land of the living."
—Psalm 52:5, 7 NIV

"He becomes poor who works with a slack and idle
hand: but the hand of the diligent makes rich."
—Proverbs 10:4 AMP

"The blessings of the Lord—it makes [truly] rich, and He adds no sorrow with it [neither does toiling increase it]."
—Proverbs 10:22 AMP

"Wealth is worthless in the day of wrath, but righteousness delivers from death."
—Proverbs 11:4 NIV

"Wealth [not earned but] won in haste or unjustly or from the production of things for detrimental use—such riches will dwindle away; but he who gathers little by little will increase his riches."
—Proverbs 13:12 AMP

"All hard work brings a profit, but mere talk leads only to poverty."
—Proverbs 14:23 NIV

"The wealth of the wise is their crown, but the folly of fools yield folly."
—Proverbs 14:24 NIV

"A man void of good sense gives a pledge and becomes security for another in the presence of his neighbor."
—Proverbs 17:18,
Proverbs 22:26

"Wealth makes many friends; the poor man is avoided by his neighbors."
—Proverbs 19:4 AMP

"Houses and riches are the inheritance from fathers."
—Proverbs 19:14 AMP

"There are precious treasures and oil in the dwelling
of the wise, but a self-confident and foolish man
swallows it up and wastes it."

—Proverbs 21:20 AMP

"Do you see a man diligent and skillful in his
business? He will stand before kings; he will not
stand before obscure men."

—Proverbs 22:29 AMP

"He that oppresses the poor to get gain for himself
and he who gives to the rich—both will surely come
to want."

—Proverbs 22:16 AMP

"He who cultivates his land will have plenty of bread,
but he who follows worthless people and pursuits will
have poverty enough."

—Proverbs 28:19 AMP

"A faithful man shall abound with blessings."

—Proverbs 28:20

"Being greedy causes strife; but he that put his trust
in the Lord shall be enriched and prosperous."

—Proverbs 28:25

"He that gives to the poor shall not lack."

— Proverbs 28:27

"Every man also to whom God hath given riches
and wealth, and hath given him power to eat thereof,
and to take his portion, and to rejoice in his labour;
this is the gift of God."

—Ecclesiastes 5:19

"Wisdom is as good as being rich; in fact, wisdom is better."

—Ecclesiastes 7:11

"...Take heed and beware of covetousness: for a man's life consisteth not in the abundance of the things which he possesseth."

—Luke 12:15

"For which of you, wishing to build a farm building, does not first sit down and calculate the cost [to see] whether he has sufficient to finish it?"

—Luke 14:28 AMP

"For you know the grace of our Lord Jesus Christ, that, though He was rich, yet for your sakes He became poor, that you through His poverty might be rich."

—2 Corinthians 8:9

"Whatever may be your task, work at it heartily (from the soul), as [something done] for the Lord and not for men. Knowing [with all certainty] that it is from the Lord [and not from men] that you will receive the inheritance which is your [real] reward."

—Colossians 3:23-34 AMP

"Charge them that are rich in this world, that they be not high-minded, nor trust in uncertain riches, but trust in the living God, who gives us richly all things to enjoy."

—1 Timothy 6:17

"Command those who are rich in this present world not to be arrogant nor to put their hope in wealth, which is so uncertain, but to put their hope in God, who richly provides us with everything for our enjoyment."
—1 Timothy 6:17 NIV

"That ye be not slothful, but followers of them who through faith and patience inherit the promises."
—Hebrews 6:12

In summary, look at what God said:

"Thus says the Lord: Let not the wise and skillful person glory and boast in his wisdom and skill; let not the mighty and powerful person glory and boast in his strength and power; let not the person who is rich [in physical gratification and earthly wealth] glory and boast in his [temporal satisfactions and earthly] riches."
—Jeremiah 9:23 AMP

As you read these scriptures, spend time meditating on them to get full revelation of what God is saying to you. Read these scriptures out loud until faith comes; they will give you a solid foundation for developing faith to possess wealth. Once you come into agreement with what God's Word says about wealth, you release your faith by thanking God for the knowledge of the truth that you were born to be wealthy.

...Oh Lord, I beseech thee, send now prosperity."
—Psalm 118:25

CHAPTER 12
FOUR WAYS TO GET RICH

Many people in today's society are looking for ways to get rich overnight. They resort to get-rich-quick schemes. The Bible has a lot to say about striving to get rich without having a relationship with the One who owns the riches. His name is Jehovah God. Without God, those with riches have no peace and they never experience everlasting joy.

One could be rich financially but spiritually bankrupt because they fail to make room for God. Those who are without God will always experience a void in their lives that only God Himself can fulfill.

The longer I live the more I realize that money can buy a lot of great things; however, money cannot buy true riches. For example, money can buy a bed, but money cannot buy you rest. Money can buy you sleeping pills, but money cannot buy peaceful sleep. Money can buy you expensive toys, but money cannot buy happiness. Here is a good one—money can buy you an elite college education, but money cannot buy you wisdom.

There are many rich and famous people in today's society who trust in their riches. God is not against us being rich; however, He is against us trusting in riches. Interestingly, the money in which people trust in constantly reminds us to trust in God. Every American currency, be it coin or dollar bills, reminds us that it is "In God We Trust."

Make sure you do not trust in and lean on your wealth and boast of the abundance of riches. Instead,

> "Trust in the Lord with all your heart; and lean not unto your own understanding. In all your ways acknowledge Him, and He shall direct your paths."
> —Proverbs 3:5-6

The following are a few ways to get rich. You make the call.

GAMBLING / WINNING THE LOTTERY

This is a form of chance and luck. Luck, in my opinion, comes from the name Lucifer—the fallen angel, Satan, the adversary, the enemy, the defeated foe. Over the years, I have seen many Christians partake in gambling. They say, "God can bless me any way He wants to." That is right—God can bless you.

God can bless you any way He wants to. The key words here are His way. God's way is sure, tried and proven. His way is not by chance, not through luck, not by your might, nor your power, but by His Spirit! God's way is not gambling, whereby you put your trust and confidence in the roll of a ball or the roll of a die or the pulling of a casino lever. This is not the way of God.

He is not the God of probabilities. He is the God of possibilities, where all things are possible with Him. I don't believe God is a God of chance and luck. The God I serve is sovereign. He is all-powerful and He knows all things. He is omniscient and omnipotent. He is the Alpha and the Omega, beginning and the end, the first and the last. (Revelation 22:13) He doesn't need to take chances at winning. He is victorious in everything and He cannot fail in anything.

I have seen the destructive and damaging effects of gambling. These "games of chance" prey on those with low income. Such prey has rapidly increased among women. Low-income mothers sometimes see gambling as a quick way to get extra money for their families.

Gambling causes people to fall into all sorts of temptations in hopes of hitting the jackpot. First Timothy 6:10 (AMP) tells us: *"For the love of money is a root of all evils; it is through this craving that some have been led astray and have wandered from the faith and pierced themselves through with many acute [mental] pangs."*

Some gamblers oftentimes sell material possessions in order to finance their gambling habits. Some gamblers even commit or contemplate committing illegal activities to fund their addictions. Studies show that gamblers tend to become unproductive workers over time and they often lead dysfunctional lives. I could go on and on regarding this subject matter. Do you get the picture?

The Lord reminds us in Proverbs 13:11 (AMP), *"Wealth [not earned but] won in haste or unjustly or from the production of things for vain or detrimental use [such riches] will dwindle away, but he who gathers little by little will increase [his riches]."*

INHERIT A LOT OF MONEY

Proverbs 20:21 (AMP) says, *"An inheritance hastily gotten [by greedy, unjust means] at the beginning, in the end it will not be blessed."* I have seen the adverse effects of people inheriting large sums of money. If they lack wisdom on how to preserve their inheritance, they end up squandering the money because they have the mind set "easy come, easy go."

A good example of one wasting their inheritance can be found in the parable of The Prodigal Son who asked for and received his inheritance prematurely.

> "And he said, A certain man had two sons: And the younger of them said to his father, Father, give me the portion of goods that falleth to me. And he divided unto them his living. And not many days after the younger son gathered all together, and took his journey into a far country, and there wasted his substance with riotous (reckless and loose) living. And when he had spent all, there arose a mighty famine in that land; and he began to be in want."
>
> —Luke 15:11-14

Godly wisdom, knowledge and understanding are essential for the preservation of the inheritance. God is not against His children receiving an inheritance. In fact, many places in the Scripture, the Lord talks about leaving and receiving an inheritance.

For example, Proverbs 19:14 tells us that houses and riches are our inheritance. As Christians, we should expect to receive inheritance. First ask yourself: "How will I handle the inheritance when I receive it? Will I spend it all and begin to be in want?" I hope not.

DO SOMETHING ILLEGAL

Another way to get rich is to do something illegal. Many people in our society who are not seeking the way of God seek this path. This path leads to death because the wages of sin is death. Proverbs 28:20 AMP reminds us that, *"A faithful man shall abound with blessings, but he who makes haste to be rich [at any cost] shall not go unpunished."*

Here are some words to the wise:

> "The earnings of the righteous (the upright, those
> who are in right standing with God) leads to life, but
> the profit of the wicked leads to further sin."
> —Proverbs 10:16 AMP

> "Let him that stole steal no more: but rather let him
> labor, working with his hands the thing which is good,
> that he may have to give to those in need."
> —Ephesians 4:28

We have recently seen an exposure of corporate leaders in America, who for years have been profiting illegally. They have gained unjustly through deception and misrepresentation of their true earnings. All must remember, whatever is done in the dark will eventually come out in the light. The prophet Jeremiah said,

> "As the partridge sitteth on eggs, and hatcheth them
> not; so he that getteth riches, and not by right, shall
> leave them in the midst of his days, and at his end
> shall be a fool."
> —Jeremiah 17:11

Don't be a fool. Be honest at all costs. Honesty, integrity and character are the ways of the Lord.

Do it God's Way

God's way is the best way! I'll say that again, God's way is the best way! Jesus said,

> " I am the way, the truth and the life."
> —John 14:6

God's way brings truth, and God's way brings life. His way has been tried and proven. His way brings good success. God's way, His ability, and His efficiency will bring you true riches, which will never fade away.

You should ask the Lord to teach you His ways. Say, "Lord, show me Your way, that I may know You." You were not created to direct your own steps. Follow God; He will lead you step by step. God wants your steps to be ordered in His Word. Ask Him to:

> "Establish my steps and direct them by [means of]
> Your word..."
> —Psalm 119:133 AMP

> "For My thoughts are not your thoughts, neither are
> your ways My ways, saith the Lord."
> —Isaiah 55:8

When you ask God to show you His way, His response is:

> "I will instruct you and teach you in the way which
> you shall go: I will guide you with My eye."
> —Psalm 32:8

Hallelujah! Furthermore, God said He is the One who enables us to profit and He who leads us by the way we should go. (Isaiah 48:17)

> "But seek (aim at and strive after) first of all His
> kingdom and His righteousness (His way of doing
> and being right), then all theses things taken together
> will be given you besides."
> —Matthew 6:33 AMP

CHAPTER 13
GOD'S WAY TO POSSESSING WEALTH

In order to have good success, make your way prosperous and possess the wealth stored up for you, it is imperative that you follow these instructions:

Meditate on God's Word

> "This book of the law shall not depart out of thy mouth; but thou shalt meditate therein day and night, that thou mayest observe to do according to all that is written therein: for then thou shalt make thy way prosperous, and then thou shall have good success."
> —Joshua 1:8

Do What God's Word Says to Do

> "My son, attend to My Words; incline your ear unto My sayings. Let them not depart from your eyes; keep them in the midst of your heart. For they are life unto those that find them, and health to all their flesh."
> —Proverbs 4:20-22

"But be ye doers of the word, and not hearers only, deceiving your own selves."

—James 1:22

Seek God

"But seek ye first the kingdom of God, and his righteousness; and all these things shall be added unto you."

—Matthew 6:33

Get Godly Counsel

"Blessed is the man that walketh not in the counsel of the ungodly, nor standeth in the way of sinners, nor sitteth in the seat of the scornful. But his delight is in the law of the LORD; and in his law doth he meditate day and night. And he shall be like a tree planted by the rivers of water, that bringeth forth his fruit in his season; his leaf also shall not wither; and whatsoever he doeth shall prosper."

—Psalm 1:1-3

Get Wisdom

"Through wisdom is a house built; and by understanding it is established: And by knowledge shall the chambers be filled with all precious and pleasant riches."

—Proverbs 24:3-4

Work Diligently

"The hand of the diligent makes rich."

—Proverbs 10:4

Recognize God's Blessings

"The blessing of the Lord makes you rich. Know that you are blessed to be a blessing."
—Proverbs 10:22;
Genesis 12:3

Give

"The generous man will be made fat—abundantly provided for."
—Proverbs 11:25

Give to the poor, widows and ministries abounding in good works.

Remain Righteous

"The righteous shall be repaid—rewarded with prosperity."
—Proverbs 13:21

Trust in the Lord

"He who trusts in the Lord shall be made fat. They shall prosper."
—Proverbs 28:25

Fear the Lord and be Humble

"The reward of humility and the reverent and worshipful fear of the Lord is riches and honor and life."
—Proverbs 22:4 AMP

Honor God With Your Wealth

> "Honor the Lord with your capital (wealth) and
> sufficiency [from righteous labors] and with the
> first fruits of all your income."
>
> —Proverbs 3:9 AMP

I believe that prior to Jesus' imminent return to catch away His glorious church out of this present world, the wealthy wicked must turn over God's wealth to God's people. With that in mind, we must be in position to receive the wealth. Once we receive the wealth, we must have godly wisdom on how to preserve and distribute the wealth. God upheld the covenant with the Israelites (those who were with God) under the old covenant. He can and He will do the same for His children today.

> "He brought them out of bondage also with silver
> and gold: and there was not one feeble person
> among their tribes. For He remembered His holy
> promise, and Abraham His servant. And He
> brought forth His people with joy, and His chosen
> with gladness: And gave them the lands of the heathen:
> and they inherited the labor of the people."
>
> —Psalm 105:37, 43- 44

God delivered on His promise to the Old Testament believers; how much more will He do it for us who have a better covenant, which was established upon better promises through Jesus our mediator?

The world must see us possessing the wealth; then they will know we are called by the name of the Lord. Then they will come asking, "What must we do to be saved?" When they see the Church of the Lord Jesus Christ in a wealthy place, then they will want our God. Go and get the wealth and lead the wicked to our covenant keeping God!

"Know therefore that the Lord thy God, he is God,
the faithful God, which keeps covenant and mercy
with them that love him and keep His commandments
to a thousand generations."
                                        —Deuteronomy 7:9

The following are ways I believe God has prescribed for us to possess
His wealth:

Tithes & Offerings
Sowing and Reaping
Saving and Investing
Working and Creating Businesses

TITHING

"Will a man rob or defraud God? Yet you rob and
defraud Me. But you say, In what way do we rob or
defraud You? [You have withheld your] tithes and
offerings. You are cursed with a curse, for you are
robbing Me, even this whole nation."
                                        —Malachi 3:8-9 AMP

I have heard many say, "How can man rob God when everything in
the earth belongs to Him? God doesn't need our money!" I have
also heard people say that tithing is for the Old Testament Church.
In Malachi 3:6, God says, *"I change not."* Can I let you in on a deep
revelation? God is not schizophrenic. God does not have a mental
disorder. He said what He meant and He means what He said.

In this scripture, the Lord is literally saying you are ripping Him off;
sticking Him up; holding Him up—taking His property unlawfully.
When you withhold your tithes, you are unjustly depriving God from
obtaining His property and His inheritance, which are lost souls.
The whole purpose for the Word of God being preached is to win

souls and grow them up in the Word of God through teaching and preaching, so they can live a victorious, radiant lifestyle and spend eternity with Almighty God.

When you withhold your tithes and offerings, fewer people get the opportunity to hear about and receive Jesus as Savior because it takes money to spread the good news of God's salvation. God gave Jesus so that He could inherit more sons and daughters. Do not rob God of His inheritance. When you do, He said you are cursing yourself twice. First, you rob God of His inheritance (people being able to hear the gospel and receive the gift of salvation) and second you rob the people who do not have the opportunity to hear God's Word. Your tithes and offerings help to spread the Gospel throughout the four corners of the world.

The tithe, or the tenth part, of all your increase does not belong to you; it belongs to God. If you allowed your best friend to wear your watch, what would you expect your friend to do after he/she was done wearing it? Return it to you, right? How would you feel or what would you think of your friend if he/she continued to wear your watch and ignored the fact that the watch did not belong to him/her?

You would probably think—the nerve of that person! He/she robbed me of my watch. This is what God says of the tithe, which belongs to Him. We tithe because we love God. We love God because He first loved us. We give offerings to show our love for and commitment to mankind.

What paying tithes and giving offerings boils down to is whether or not you believe the Word of God. I am a living witness that giving tithes and offerings has wonderful, supernatural benefits that money cannot buy.

If you have not committed to tithing, I encourage you to do so. It pays to pay your tithes.

> "Bring all the tithes (the whole tenth of your income)
> into the storehouse, that there may be food in My house
> (The Church of the Lord), and prove Me now by it, says
> the Lord of hosts, if I will not open the windows of
> heaven for you and pour you out a blessing, that there
> shall not be room enough to receive it."
> —Malachi 3:10 AMP

Notice this scripture does not say tithing would put meat in your house; that is what the 90 percent is for—the needs of your house. Tithing brings meat into God's house to meet the needs of His people through ministering His Word.

When the Lord said He would open the windows of heaven and pour you out a blessing, that does not mean He will literally pour money from heaven. He is saying that He will empower you to prosper in such a way that you won't have room enough to receive it.

We have a blessed assurance that tithing connects us to God's efficiency. God's efficiency allows us to prosper financially, spiritually, mentally and physically. We get a wonderful package deal when we tithe! Not only are we blessed, but others are also given the opportunity to be blessed.

As I stated earlier, some would say tithing was for the Old Testament Church. No. Tithing is very much still a part of our modern Church. Jesus cannot return until everyone gets an opportunity to hear the good news. Matthew 24:14: *"And this gospel of the kingdom shall be preached in all the world for a witness unto all nations; and then shall the end come."*

It may surprise you to note that even today our tithes are received by the One who lives perpetually. His name is Jesus. (Hebrews 7:8) Yes, Jesus is still receiving our tithes. Jesus Himself said,

> "It is more blessed to give than to receive."
> —Acts 20:35

When you receive, that's it. The blessing is over. On the other hand, as you give and give and give, it is given back to you infinitely.

This is why the Lord says to bring your tithes and prove Him, try Him, test Him and see if He will not pour you out or empty out to you a liberal pool of prosperity so much so that you do not have enough room or space to receive it. This sounds like guaranteed blessings. Tithing is a great exchange!

Remember the Lord said to bring a tenth of your increase; this means you tithe from your gross income, not your net income (the amount after taxes.) God said to give him your first fruits. (Proverbs 3:9) That means God gets His tithe and offerings before Uncle Sam the taxman gets his.

I caution you not to consider that you are giving the preacher the money to make him and his family rich. When you give, you are giving to God to help the poor—the spiritually poor, the physically poor, the emotionally poor and so on.

God said when you give to the poor you are giving to Him and He will repay you. (Proverbs 19:17) Therefore, do not worry about the kind of car the preacher drives. Do not concern yourself with what kind of house they live in or the clothes they wear. Jesus is the One who receives your tithes and offerings. (Hebrews 7:8)

Do you not know that those men (mankind) who are employed in the services of the temple (church) get their food from the temple?

And that those who tend the altar share with the altar [in the offerings brought]? [On that same principle] the Lord directed that those who publish the good news (the Gospel) should live (get their maintenance) by the Gospel. (1 Corinthians 9:13-14 AMP)

When you give, give out of love. Do not give out of necessity or grudgingly. God loves a cheerful and prompt giver. (2 Corinthians 9:7) When you give, God said it will be given back to you. Your giving causes you to be blessed. When the poor hear the teaching and preaching of the Word, they are also blessed.

> "Let him who receives instruction in the Word [of God] share all good things with his teacher [contributing to his support]."
>   —Galatians 6:6 AMP

SOWING AND REAPING

In the original Hebrew and Greek texts, to *"sow"* means: *to disseminate, scatter, plant or conceive seed.* Likewise, to **"reap"** means: *to harvest, cut and gather.* Sowing and reaping is an excellent principle God has established to allow us to walk in the overflow of His blessings.

Sowing seeds is not limited to giving monetarily. Sowing seeds could also entail volunteering your time to help someone, doing something nice for someone such as baby-sitting, running an errand, giving a compliment, etc. This list could go on and on.

Sow your time, talent and finances as unto the Lord. Sow into good ground—ministries committed to preaching and teaching the infallible Word of God. Sow into ministries that are committed to going into the entire world to preach the Gospel of our Lord and Savior, Jesus the Anointed One.

What do you need in your life? Sow a seed. Philippians 4:19 says: *"But my God shall supply all your need according to His riches in glory by Christ Jesus."* Prior to this statement being made, the Apostle Paul was speaking to a group of believers who were committed to giving to his ministry. These believers sowed seed into his ministry once and again. Because they were givers, God said He would meet their needs. There is a connection between giving and having all of your needs met. Think about that.

God gave us this example for us to follow. Everything God does comes from a seed. In Genesis 8:22 He says, *" While the earth remains, seedtime and harvest, and cold and heat, and summer and winter, and day and night shall not cease."*

You will reap what you sow. When you sow a seed, you should expect to receive. As you read this, you may be thinking, "I sow all the time and I am waiting on my harvest." It may appear that only the sinners are reaping where they haven't sown. Look at what God said in Amos 9:13: *"Behold, the days come, says the Lord, that the plowman shall overtake the reaper."*

> "And let us not be weary in well doing: for in due
> season we shall reap, if we faint not."
> —Galatians 6:9

Your harvest time will come! Continue to sow and wait expectantly for an extraordinary God to do extraordinary things in your life.

Keep sowing and expect to reap. Continue to put God in remembrance of the seeds you have sown and expect your return.Wait eagerly and expectantly for the Ephesians 3:20 God—the One who is able to bless you super-abundantly, far over and above all that you can ever ask or think, infinitely beyond your highest prayers, your highest desires, your highest thoughts, hopes or dreams! (AMP) God Loves a Cheerful Giver! Sow sparingly, you will reap sparingly; sow bountifully, you will reap bountifully; sow according as you have purposed in your heart; do not give out of necessity, regretfully, or because of pressure for God loves a cheerful, prompt to do giver. (2 Corinthians 9:6-7)

What Happens When You Give Cheerfully?

> "And God is able to make all grace abound toward you; that you always having all sufficiency in all things may abound to every good work."
>
> —2 Corinthians 9:8

> "Give, and it shall be given unto you; good measure, pressed down, and shaken together, and running over, shall men give into your bosom. For with the same measure that ye mete withal it shall be measured to you again."
>
> —Luke 6:38

GIVE YOUR BEST

In Genesis 4:3-5 we see two brothers giving to God. The scripture says God had respect and regard for Abel's offering but had no respect or regard for Cain's offering. The reason God had respect and regard for Abel's offering is because *"Abel brought of the firstlings of his flock AND of the fat thereof."* Abel gave God his firstfruits, which was his tithe. In addition, he gave an offering out of the fat—the extra or the surplus he had in his possession.

On the other hand, Cain simply gave an offering. This wasn't Cain's best. He did not honor the Lord with his firstfruits. As a result, God was not impressed. God expects us to honor Him with the firstfruits of all our increase. (Proverbs 3:9) God gave His best. He gave us Jesus. God gave us His best so that we could have the good, abundant, God kind of life here on earth. Give Your Best!

GIVE TO THE POOR

"For ye know the grace of our Lord Jesus Christ, that, though he was rich, yet for your sakes he became poor, that ye through his poverty might be rich."
—2 Corinthians 8:9

"He that giveth to the poor shall not lack: but he that hideth his eyes shall have many a curse."
—Proverbs 28:27

"He that hath pity upon the poor lends unto the LORD; and that which he hath given will he pay him again."
—Proverbs 19:17

"Blessed is he who considers the poor and those in need; the Lord will deliver him in time of trouble. The Lord will preserve him and keep him alive, and he will be blessed on the earth."
—Psalm 41:1-2

"Give to him that asks thee, and from him that would borrow of thee turn not thou away."
—Matthew 5:42

"He who oppresses the poor reproaches, mocks, and insults his Maker, but he who is kind and merciful to the needy honors Him."
—Proverbs 14:31 AMP

"Rob not the poor because he is poor."
—Proverbs 22:22

"Is it not to divide your bread with the hungry and
bring the homeless poor into your house—when you
see the naked, that you cover him, and that you hide
not yourself from [the needs of] your own flesh and
blood."

—Isaiah 58:7 AMP

"They only [made one stipulation] that we were to
remember the poor, which very thing I was also eager
to do."

—Galatians 2:10 AMP

SAVING AND INVESTING

The first and foremost example of God's method of investing is in
tithes and offerings. When we give our tithes and offerings, we are
investing into the kingdom of God. Our investment multiplies each
time someone hears the gospel. Your return on your investment
comes in the form of God's unspeakable gifts and benefits, which He
provides you with daily.

God's original intent was for His children to increase or multiply the
monies given to them by saving and investing (See Luke 19:15-26).
In fact, you will find that God is disappointed in the individual who
does not seek to invest his or her supply. God calls such a person a
wicked servant.

The whole concept of investing money works well when people
deal honestly and with integrity. Unfortunately, today's investment
market conditions have been tainted with inside trading scandals
and numerous dishonest, deceptive dealings, all of which are driven
by fear and greed.

Recently, USA Today News reported that a large New York financial
institution agreed to pay $50 million to settle charges of abusive

mutual funds sales and practices.[2]   It is unfortunate that honest investors are impacted by such insidious practices. This is why it is so important that you do not trust in uncertain riches. Before you invest in the market, it is important that you get godly counsel.

I have heard people say investing is just like gambling. That is not true. When an individual gambles, generally, one person wins the big jackpot. However, when individuals invest, and if there is a profit to be made, everyone profits from the return on their investment. There is a big difference. Investing is not gambling or speculation. Investing is taking pre-determined risks to earn steady rewards. Investing allows you to participate in the relentless growth of the world's economy.

Although investment growth does not go in a straight line, generally you will see upward trends over time. In many cases, the longer you stay in your investment, the greater your return. The concept called compounding is a mathematical certainty, which affords investors a good return on their investments. Compounding is a method of computing interest where your money increases based on the principal (original amount invested) and the accrued (gained) interest.

Studies have shown that in order to keep up with the rate of inflation, one must direct his or her money towards investment products that will produce a rate of return that will hedge against inflation. For example, when I was seven years old, a McDonalds hamburger cost approximately 25 cents. Today, that same hamburger costs approximately 70 cents.

The increase in cost is known as inflation. If your savings account is paying you a two percent rate of interest and the inflation rate is three percent, you will not have sufficient money to keep up with the increasing cost of living. Therefore, many people look for a diversity of investment tools to help grow their money.

There are numerous types of savings and investment tools to choose from; however, I will discuss some of the most widely used. Following are examples of savings and investments vehicles which can get you on the road to accumulation and preservation of wealth:

Regular Savings Account: May be establish for an indefinite period. You have access to the account at all times. You may make deposits or withdrawals at anytime. The interest rates are usually very low and are set by the financial institution. There is no risk involved and this is a safe way to save. Typically, the FDIC (Federal Deposit Insurance Corporation) insures your savings account up to $100,000.

Money Market Account: An account with no regulated minimum term and with unrestricted deposits. You are allowed six pre-authorized or automatic fund transfers per month, no more than three transfers by check. The initial deposit is $2,500. If your balance falls below $2,500, your account will be assessed a maintenance fee. Interest rates are sometimes tiered based on your balance, which means the more you have on deposit, the higher the interest rate. This is a good place to put your money between investments.

Time Deposit: Another type of savings account which pays interest for a set time-frame at a set or variable rate of interest. In many instances, the amount and length of time you are investing will determine your rate. A minimum investment is usually $1,000; some institutions offer opening deposits as low as $500. There is generally a penalty for early withdrawals since the savings agreement calls for investing the money for a specified time—generally from 30 days to 10 years.

Certificate of Deposit: Often used interchangeably with Time Deposit; however there are differences. The minimum deposit for a jumbo certificate of deposit is $100,000 and the interest rate can be negotiated. The length of time for investing is usually anywhere from seven days to 365 days. Generally, there is a penalty for early withdrawal.

Individual Retirement Account (IRA): A tax-deferred savings vehicle used for retirement planning. IRAs are governed by tax laws, which change often. A basic premise is that annual contributions can be made for 100% of earned income up to a maximum of $2000. These contributions can be made until a person reaches 70½. At that time, the individual must take mandatory distributions based on life expectancy. There are many types of IRA plans available. Visit your local bank for brochures which will enlighten you on the various types.

Retail Repurchase Agreement (REPO): An agreement between a customer (individual or business) and a financial institution where the institution sells a portion of their securities portfolio, which primarily consists of government securities. The institution agrees to pay a specific rate of interest for a specific length of time. Once that time-period is up, the institution repurchases the security from the customer.

Most institutions require a minimum investment of $1 million. However, there are instances where they will accept a lesser amount and combine your agreement with another to reach the $1 million mark. These investments can be made for a time-period as short as one day and up to 90 days. The advantage of this type of investment is a higher rate of interest.

Sweep Account: An account that links a low interest or a non-interest account with an investment account, which earns a higher rate of interest. The account is called a "sweep" because it sweeps idle balances over a targeted amount into the investment account. If the balance in the low interest account falls below the target balance, funds are swept back into that account. Many businesses and individual account holders use this type of account to maximize their idle balances. The interest rates are typically competitive in the sweep account.

Keogh Plan: An account which allows self-employed and non-incorporated individuals to save money for retirement. This is a qualified tax-deferred savings plan. This plan has maximum salaries on which employer contributions may be based. Employers who establish a plan must make the plan available to their qualified employees.

401K: A federally regulated pre-tax savings contribution made through your employer. This is a good way to save because your contribution comes out of your pay before taxes are taken out. Many companies offer "matching contributions" where your employer will match, sometimes, up to six percent of your annual income. This is free money! The interest earned is tax deferred until you make withdrawals. This is a benefit worth looking into. For more information, see the benefit representative at your job or your financial advisor.

WORKING & CREATING BUSINESSES

Do you see a man diligent and skillful (any truly competent workers) in his business? He will stand before kings; he will not stand before obscure (ordinary) men. (Proverbs 22:29 AMP)

Another part of God's plan for you to possess wealth can be accomplished by working. Your work, your job, your vocation, or whatever you want to call what you do—your work is your business.

The Bible says if you don't work you don't eat. (2 Thessalonians 3:10) Growing up, I would often hear adults say, "The only place where success comes before work is in the dictionary." They were right! Scripture tells us:

"He becomes poor who works with a slack and idle hand,
but the hand of the diligent maketh rich."
—Proverbs 10:4 AMP

Your blessings come with doing what God has called you to do.
Everyone has work to do. Get this revelation; God cannot bless your
work if you are not doing your work.

"Be ye strong therefore, and let not your hands be weak:
for your work shall be rewarded."
—2 Chronicles 15:7

"The LORD rewarded me according to my righteousness:
according to the cleanness of my hands hath he
recompensed (to pay/reward) me."
—2 Samuel 22:21

"The soul of a sluggard (lazy person) desireth, and
hath nothing: but the soul of the diligent shall be
made fat (abundantly supplied)."
—Proverbs 13:4

"And whatsoever ye do, do it heartily, as unto the Lord,
and not unto men. Knowing that of the Lord ye shall
receive the reward of the inheritance."
—Colossians 3:23-24

"Lazy hands make a man poor, but diligent hands
bring wealth."
—Proverbs 10:4 NIV

Too often, we look for "pie in the sky" or "get-rich-quick" schemes.
Don't get me wrong, I believe in miracles. I fully believe the biblical
story of Jesus and Peter paying their taxes with "miracle money"

which came from the mouth of a fish. (Matthew 17:27) While it was a miracle that a fish would have money in his mouth, Peter still had to go fishing in order to get the money out of the mouth of the fish. Peter had to do something to get the money.

Likewise, when Jesus "called" His disciples, they were all working and left their work to follow Jesus. Clearly, working is a pathway to possessing wealth. A major way to create wealth is through business ownership. Being an entrepreneur can be an exciting and rewarding experience. Recognize however, that the road to becoming a successful business owner can be challenging; but it can be done!

In the first part of the book, I discussed at length, the spiritual aspects of possessing wealth. In the second part of the book, I want to discuss in detail, financial insights regarding wealth accumulation and wealth preservation. I will also share practical principles on how to start a business, as well as how to manage your finances both personally and professionally.

PART II

"No servant is able to serve two masters; for either he will hate the one and love the other, or he will stand by and be devoted to the one and despise the other. You cannot serve God and mammon (riches, or anything in which you trust and on which you rely)."

—Luke 16:13 (AMP)

CHAPTER 14
BECOMING AN ENTREPRENEUR

Ask any reputable financial consultant to describe the portrait of a millionaire and his or her response might be, "the average self-made millionaire is a middle-aged (or older) person who drives a car in the average price range; has been married to the same person for more than 20 years; goes to church; owns or runs a business; has kids; works a 10-hour day and loves it." You have just read the description of a "self-made" millionaire. Can you imagine what a "God-made" millionaire might look like?

God is no respecter of persons. What He has done for others, He can do for you. You can possess God's wealth and achieve success over time by working diligently and by trusting God to bless the work of your hands. Although entrepreneurial work can be challenging, the rewards are endless. Let's take a look at the steps to becoming an entrepreneur.

STEPS TO ENTREPRENEURSHIP

Contact your local Small Business Development Center. They can assist you in planning for and managing your business success. As a business owner, some of the things you will need to consider are as follows:

- **Writing Your Business Plan**
- **Financing Your Business**
- **Marketing Your Business**
- **Choosing Your Business Structure**
- **Licenses, Permits and other regulations**
- **Employees**
- **Taxes and Insurance**
- **Bookkeeping**

One of the first things you should do before going into business is pray. Ask God for His ideal business for you. A God idea is far better than a good idea. Next, complete a feasibility study. This study will help to determine the present and future need for the type of business you are considering. This is a very important step which should not be overlooked.

One thing I have learned about hearing God's instructions is the importance of timing. Proper timing will make the difference between success and failure. God may give you a great business idea; however, you must know the proper time to implement the God idea.

"To everything there is a season."
—Ecclesiastes 3:1

HOW TO START A BUSINESS

- **Select a business idea** (Seek God for a "God Idea")
- **Investigate sources of assistance**
- **Research your market**
- **Determine and register legal structure**
- **Determine tax obligations**
- **Identify location of business**
- **Determine need for business insurance**
- **Determine whether or not you will hire employees**
- **Identify major suppliers**

- Develop a forecast of financial needs
- Identify source of funds
- Establish a bookkeeping system
- Select a bank that understands your business

Incorporate all of this information into a business plan. A business plan can provide you with a pathway to profitability. It can help you focus on critical questions which must be answered if your business is going to thrive and grow.

A good business plan produces a working document that can help you accomplish your goals. A successful plan communicates the following information clearly and concisely:

- **The nature of your business**
- **Your mission statement**
- **The goals and objectives of your business**
- **The steps you need to take to achieve your goals and objectives**
- **An action plan for implementing these steps**
- **Major potential problems and strategies for overcoming these problems**
- **Your potential customers**
- **How you will market to potential customers**
- **The principal participants in your business**
- **The current financial resources of your company**

HOW TO REGISTER YOUR BUSINESS

The legal structure of your business is very important. I suggest that you get counsel on the best way to set up your business. The following chart on the next page is simply a brief description of some of the ways you can set up the legal structure of your business:

TYPE OF BUSINESS	OWNERSHIP	WHO WILL CONTROL?	OWNER LIABILITY	TAXATION
Sole Proprietor-ship	Individually owned	Owner will control	Owner is personally liable for all debts.	Income from the business is considered personal income to the owner and is taxed at the going personal tax rates.
General Partnership	Partnership agreement is established between two or more individuals	Partners control according to partnership agreement	Partners are equally held liable for all partnership debts.	Partners share profits or losses which is included on their personal tax returns. Each partner is taxed at their respective personal tax rates.
Limited Partnership	Two or more owners who classify themselves as general or limited partners	General partners may close the business using their judgment. Limited partners cannot make this decision. General partners are the ones who run the business according to the partnership agreement.	General partners are fully responsible for all business debts, while the limited partner is only liable in comparison to the amount of capital invested.	Taxation is the same as the general partnership (above).
"C" Corporation	Has an unlimited number of shareholders	Ownership is shared among owners through stock purchase. The business is managed through an established Board of Directors with certain legal regulations having being established.	Owners held responsible to the amount of capital they invested unless they were a guarantor of corporate debt.	Corporation pay taxes based on business income at the established corporate rate. Profits are distributed to shareholders and the shareholders are taxed at their respective personal income tax rate.
"S" Subchapter Corporation	Has 35 or less shareholders	Same as "C" corporation above	Same as "C" Corporation; however liability is limited to the corporation's assets.	No taxes for corporation. Shareholders are taxed at personal income tax rate.

PLACES TO GO FOR HELP

"...You have not because you ask not..."
                                    —James 4:3

Before starting your business, you will need to be diligent in researching the God idea and find out what it will take to make your business grow to the glory of God. You will need to talk to experts and use different resources to help start your business. Most of the external resources are free of charge, while others may charge a fee.

The following is a short list of places where you can go for expert help:

Small Business Development Center
Most cities have a small business development network which consists of counseling and service centers dedicated to providing no-charge management and technical assistance to current and future business owners. Some service centers are designed to do such things as:

Help minorities, women, the handicapped, veterans, and other groups with special needs, which will help them overcome obstacles and help them build a successful business.

Help with writing business plans, gaining access to financing, marketing strategies, accounting, bookkeeping, inventory control and much more.

Provide one-on-one counseling to small business owners.

Offer educational programs tailored to the needs of the business owner.

Chamber of Commerce

Each city should have a local Chamber of Commerce, which can be a good source for information concerning the city's ordinances and demographics This type of information will be helpful in running your business operation. This is also a great place to meet the movers and shakers in your respective community. Generally, chamber meetings are held on a monthly basis.

Libraries

I cannot say enough about the importance of utilizing the library—both public and those on university campuses. The library offers a wealth of information on everything you need to know about business. The reference section in most libraries offers periodicals with information on a number of industries.

You will also find a large assortment of books on marketing, financing, and growing your business. There are even books on how to read financial statements.

Professionals

You will need a team of professionals in order to have a successful business. Just as you need a doctor, barber, hair stylist, cleaners and/or grocery store—you will need a team of professionals.

Every business should have a good bank, a knowledgeable banker, reputable lawyer, trustworthy certified public accountant, and a good insurance agent. Of course, the prerequisite for your team of professionals is that they must use godly wisdom, or your business will not be "blessed." (See Psalm 1:1)

Do not expect these professionals to counsel you free of charge. If you are going to get the best counsel, you will pay accordingly. Always remember, you get what you pay for. Don't worry; in the long run, the fees paid to these professionals will pay for themselves.

Trade Associations

Trade associations are a great source of information concerning the ins and outs of your type of business because they show you what's going on in your industry and what special challenges you could possibly face. To find your trade association, go to the library and check the Encyclopedia of Associations. This information can be found in the reference section of most libraries.

Banks

Of course, I am partial to banks, having been a banker for more than 17 years. Here you will find a lot of information on topics ranging from financial services tailor made to help you manage your business to providing private banking services. Many banks cater to small businesses. Oftentimes they provide workshops designed to help you succeed in business and the cost for these workshops is usually nominal. Be sure to establish a good relationship with your banker. A good banker is essential to succeeding in business.

HOW TO FINANCE YOUR BUSINESS

"For which of you, intending to build a tower, sitteth not down first, and counteth the cost, whether he have sufficient to finish it?"
—Luke 14:28

Once you have a God idea, you must seek God for His plan on how you should finance the business. God said He will perfect everything that concerns you (Psalm 138:8); this includes how to finance your business.

There are many ways to accomplish this. What's important is doing it God's way. When we do our part, God will do His part. In other words, when we do what we know to do in the natural, God will add His "super" and in the end we know God's way is always supernatural!

One of the most dangerous mistakes made in launching a new business is not having a realistic approach in the area of finances. Many businesses do not plan to fail and often fail because they did not pre-determine how much money would be needed to sustain the business in a worst-case scenario. Remember, "if you fail to plan, you plan to fail."

Having sufficient finances to support your business could make the difference between whether or not your business succeeds or fails. With that said, it is critically important that you determine the financial needs of your business and the options for financing your business. The following is a guide to help you decide.

DETERMINING YOUR START-UP NEEDS

You will need to identify all costs associated with starting your business. Some of these will be a one-time cost while others will be fixed, ongoing costs. The key here is "less is best." Only incur costs which are bare necessities when launching your business.

Your fixed costs, or overhead costs, are those such as utilities, inventory, taxes, etc. You will also have various other administrative costs. You must be able to cover these costs, even if your projected sales/profits are not coming in as quickly as you anticipated.

If you are not sure how to do a cash flow projection, learn how to do so. This type of analysis will help you determine how much you will need to start up your business and how much money you will need to generate in order for your business to survive. Ideally, you want to strive for your cash in-flow to be greater than your out-flow. Realistically, when starting a new business, you are doing well to break even.

DETERMINE YOUR FINANCING OPTIONS

The next thing you will need to do is determine which financing vehicle is best for you. Even when you have identified your source, always have a backup plan. The following are a few sources to consider:

Using Personal Funds: This is probably the most common source for funding a new business venture. Oftentimes people borrow funds from friends and family or they use their own personal funds. For example, Mr. Sanders used his social security check to start Kentucky Fried Chicken®. In some instances, homeowners use equity in their home, or they borrow against or sell other assets to get the required funds to start the business.

Using Private Investors: Some people use private investors to finance their start-up costs. This kind of financing can be accomplished in many ways, from establishing a general partnership to having a private or public stock offering. You will need a competent, God-fearing financial professional, such as a Certified Public Accountant (CPA), for advice concerning the rules and regulations centered around this option.

Using Financial Institutions: It has been my experience that banks and other financial institutions generally do not finance start-up expenses, primarily because lending to a start-up business is a big risk. Banks are very conservative when lending money and therefore tend to pass on these opportunities. Banks do not like to lend to new business ventures that do not have any proven track record, because the money banks lend belongs to their depositors and they must protect their depositor's interest.

Using Venture Capitalists: Venture capitalists invest in your business and become co-owners with you. They will sometimes take an active role in managing your company. Frequently, they ask for a controlling interest in your business. Venture capitalists look for a high return on their investment (usually several hundred percent) over a relatively short period of time (usually between three to five years). After this period of time they tend to expect you or someone else to buy them out.

This list of options is not all-inclusive. For assistance in exploring the various financing options, contact your local Small Business Development Center.

How to Market Your Business

Even the best product or service in the world does not automatically guarantee success. In order for you to grow, potential customers must be informed about your product/service, and they must purchase those products and services. Developing and implementing a marketing strategy is paramount to the success of your business. The following is a guide to marketing your business:

Identify The Product or Service You Really Sell: Focus on your market niche. Specifically, what needs are you fulfilling by offering your product or service? For example, a hair salon owner not only offers hair artistry; they could also offer make-up products, nail care, image consulting, jewelry, refreshments, etc. The needs being fulfilled there is "one-stop shopping." A client could: get their hair and nails done, their eyebrows waxed, buy fashion accessories and get their feet cared for at the same place where they have access to snacks.

Identify Potential Clients: Your potential clients are those who you will cater to by fulfilling their specific needs with your products or services. In turn, you must determine who those clients are that will consider using your business based on your prices, location, quality of product and other determining factors. Remember that everyone is not your client. You will need to focus on a realistic target group within the marketplace.

Know Your Competitors: Your competitors are primarily those who are fulfilling the same needs you are satisfying. They may or may not be in the same business as your business; however, they offer the same products/services as you do. For example, companies providing guard services to warehouses and those selling alarm systems to warehouses are competitors, although they are not in the same industry.

Chapter 15
DEVELOPING YOUR GOD-GIVEN GIFT

K eep in mind that everyone is not "called" to be a business owner. However, everyone has a divine invitation from God to do something specific here in the earth. God created you for an intended purpose and placed inside of you special gifts and endowments to do great things in the earth.

Everything God created was for His pleasure (Revelation 4:11). It is important that you seek God to find out for yourself what He created you to do and do that, because only what you do for Christ, will last. Find out what gifts He has given to you, so that you can make a major contribution to society.

Before the foundations of this earth, you and I were created to complete a specific plan from God. Find out God's plan for your life and follow His plan.   Everything God created was to solve a problem, you included. For example, the stove was created to cook; the light bulb was created to give off light; the clock was created to tell time; shoes were created to protect feet—and so on. What has God created you to do?

Take the time to find out what problem(s) God created you to solve. Look at the major contribution Bill Gates is making to revolutionize the world. He has taken computer technology to another level, so much so that the Government has tried to break up his power of dominating in this area of technology.

Think about the numerous inventions given to man by God. We are benefiting from these products and services because someone discovered their call and their gift. Here are some examples:

The person who invented bottled water. Who would have thought we would be paying for water over the counter?

The person who invented the Chip Clip® simply used the wisdom of God and transferred an old fashioned clothespin into a Chip Clip®.

What about the people who came up with the WWJD® (What Would Jesus Do) slogan plastered on wristbands, key chains, tee shirts, etc?

I think about the person who came up with liquid shoe polish.

What about the person who got the idea to make chewing gum?

Look at the wisdom God gave Garrett A. Morgan who invented the traffic signal, the gas mask and the sewing machine zigzag attachment.

I could go on and on! Why can't God use you to make a major impact on society for generations to come? God can and He will use you to do mighty things in the earth! It is up to you, however, to find out your gift and your call. You are responsible for seeking God for that revelation.

In the meantime, ask yourself the following questions: What do I love to do to such an extent that I would be willing to do it for free? What am I good at doing? What am I passionate about? What works my nerves? What do I see happening in the world that makes me hurt deep down inside?

The answers to these questions may be an indication of God's gift *(miraculous faculty or an endowment)* and calling *(invitation)*.

> "God's gifts and calling are without repentance."
> —Romans 11:29

Once God gives gifts, He does not take them back. It is up to you to broaden your horizon. Begin to think big. After all, we serve a big God. It's time to take God out of the box. Our limited, small thinking limits God's ability to perform big miracles in our lives.

Begin to cry out to God for discoveries and inventions. Ask the Lord to put wisdom and understanding into your heart to know how to work all manner of work—whatever He has created you to do.

> "The counsel (purpose) in the heart of man is like water in a deep well, but a man of understanding draws it out."
> —Proverbs 20:5

YOUR GIFT IS TIED TO YOUR WEALTH

On September 5, 2002 in the wee hours of the morning, I was wide-awake, so I went into my secret place to seek the Lord. God said those who seek Him, will find Him. As I was praying in the Spirit, I received the following instructions, which I believe will set you on your course to possessing the wealth:

Develop Your Thought Life! While I have mentioned this before, this concept bears repeating. When the people were building the Tower of Babel in Genesis Chapter 11, they were able to accomplish something new that no one had done in the past. The architectural design and the process used to make the bricks to construct the tower was never used before this time. God said of these people,

> "nothing that they have imagined shall be impossible
> for them."
>
> —Genesis 11:6 AMP

Although these people were building the tower out of disobedience to God, their thought-life produced an end result. When we think on those things that are honest and pure, God will *do exceeding, abundantly above all we ask or think* (Ephesians 3:20).

Think of or Imagine What You Can do to Accumulate Wealth. Once you have thought about this, no less than one hour, write it down! Did you know you earn money by using your brain? I heard Peter Daniels, a Christian billionaire, say—stop being a workaholic and become a think-aholic! Therein lies a passport to possessing the wealth. Our brain is one of the most powerful computers in the earth, yet we only use 10 percent of it.

Think About The Garden of Eden, which was known as the Garden God planted. This garden was a place of wealth, delight, paradise, and pleasure. The literal translation of the term "Garden of Eden" means to "live in luxury." From the beginning of time, God's will for His children was for them to live in their wealthy place; to live in delight; to live in paradise, and to live in pleasure. The Garden of Eden is also illustrated as the greatest prosperity God would bestow on His people Judah (Christians from the tribe of Judah). This Garden was also a symbol of blessing and bounty. (Isaiah 51:3; Ezekiel 36:35)

Imagine Having Four Income Streams. If you were to think about and examine how the wealthy possessed their wealth, you would find that most accumulated their wealth through multiple income streams. Multiple income streams can make your dreams of possessing wealth come true.

"For a dream cometh through the multitude of business."
—Ecclesiastes 5:3

Imagine a Teenager With Four Income Streams. Yes! That is possible. What you think cannot be done, someone else is already doing it. For example, a 16 year-old could have a summer job, rake leaves in the fall and shovel snow in the winter. He or she could then invest a minimum of 30 percent of his or her earnings. The interest income from the investment becomes the fourth source of income.

This is just a thought; however, I would like to encourage teens reading this book to become more creative by learning various ways to produce income. Get into practice now so that when you reach adulthood you can take your income producing method to the next level.

Think on This! Your Wealth is Tied to Your Streams of Income. The Garden of Eden had four streams of water leading to it.

"Now a river went out of Eden to water the garden; and from there it divided and became four [river] heads."
—Genesis 2:10 AMP

In order for the garden to grow and continue to be nourished, an abundant supply of water was needed. One of the four streams of water surrounded the —

"...land of Havilah, where their is gold. The gold of that land is of high quality; bdellium (pearl) and onyx stone are there."
—Genesis 2:11-12 AMP

Think on this: your streams of income will allow you to possess the wealth.

Imagine This! God **Has Not** changed His mind.

> "I am the Lord, I change not.
> —Malachi 3:6

The Lord said the earth is His and the fullness thereof. Then He said He gave the earth to the children of men. (Psalm 24:1; Psalm 115:16) God has given us a wealthy place. Now it's time to possess the wealth! That is one of the reasons God sent Jesus—to restore us back to the position of wealth and authority where Adam and Eve once were. Jesus did His part; now it is time to do your part. Possess God's wealth!

Imagine That There is a Great Gift Inside You, Which Will Take You to Your Wealthy Place. Stir up the gift God placed inside you! Stop allowing your gift to lay dormant; stir it up! God has put inside you the wisdom and understanding needed to live a victorious life. A victorious life is a good life.

God has given each of us various abilities which, when discovered and mastered, can bring us to a place of wealth. One good example is a professional athlete. Can you imagine doing something you love doing and getting paid lots of money to do it? The gift that will take you to the wealthy place is something you love to do with such passion that you would be willing to do it free of charge.

What is your passion? What is your gift? The most precious gift we have on the inside is the Gift of the Holy Spirit. God Himself lives inside of you. Greatness is inside of you! Begin to utilize your Gift!

Seek God and ask the Holy Spirit to help you and show you how to bring this mission of possessing His wealth to pass. Set aside time to listen to God's response. Make an appointment to meet with God to get your life-changing instructions.

If you are serious about hearing from God, I would suggest scheduling your appointment for no less than 1 hour. This is not a one-time process. Those who seek the Lord shall not lack anything that is good. Once you receive your instructions, write them down and do what God tells you to do! Do it now! The greatest deception the devil uses is procrastination—putting off what can be done today for tomorrow. Remember, the hand of the diligent makes rich (Proverbs 10:4). Become diligent in doing what God told you to do. Just do it! Do it now!

CHAPTER 16
MONEY TALKS!

I want to speak in brief about the subject of money. **Webster's New Riverside Dictionary** defines *"money"* as: *paper or metal currency that is officially established as being exchangeable for goods and services; currency issued by a government; wealth and affluence considered in terms of its monetary value.*

There are three important components to money. I call them the *"three S's"*: Share some. Spend some. Lastly, Save some. Unfortunately, most people do more spending than sharing and saving. The society in which we live is one where we are prone to consuming trillions of dollars annually on goods and services. Clearly, we need to find a balance between sharing, spending and saving.

Being a good steward by applying the *"three S's"* of money is essential to accumulating wealth. It is critically important that every household have a savings plan. A working individual should have in liquid savings at least three to six month's income set aside in the event of an emergency. When I say liquid, I mean those funds should be readily available to meet the need of any unforeseen expenses.

To accomplish this, you must first pay your tithes and then pay yourself. Once you have a solid savings plan in place, then you can begin to invest the surplus of money you may have.

Money, which is the driving force behind wealth, is simply a medium of exchange for goods and services. We have seen in God's Word that money answers all things and that money is a defense. (Ecclesiastes 7:12; 10:19) Needless to say, money plays an important role in life in general. As a result, I believe it is a God idea to intercede and supplicate in prayer for those who are in charge of our Nation's money supply—The Federal Reserve Board.

The primary function of the Federal Reserve Board is to oversee the Nation's banking system. The governing body consists of seven Board of Governors who are appointed by the President of the United States and confirmed by the Senate to serve a 14-year term.

This board assists the U.S. Government in managing the economy by encouraging economic growth and controlling inflation, primarily by influencing interest rates and the availability of MONEY and loans. The current Chairman of the Board is Alan Greenspan, and the Vice Chairman is Alice Rivlin.

God instructs us in 1 Timothy 2:1-2 to make: *supplications, prayers, intercessions, and giving of thanks for all men; for kings, and for all that are in authority.* Why? So that we may lead a quiet and peaceable life in all godliness and honesty. Can you imagine what it would be like if all the wealth in the earth was equally shared? Everyone would be wealthy!

Pray that the Chairman and Vice Chairman, along with the other five board members, will be surrounded with godly wisdom; that their eyes will be flooded with the light of the Gospel. Pray that the Father of glory may give to them the spirit of wisdom and revelation in the knowledge of Him; the eyes of their understanding being enlightened; that they may know what is the hope of His calling, and what the riches of the glory of His inheritance in the saints. (Ephesians 1:17-18)

Pray! When we pray for others, God's plan for all men to be saved and to come to the knowledge of the truth will be fulfilled. Prayer changes things!

I also believe it is a God idea to know the U.S. currency. As mentioned before, on the front of all U.S. currency, both paper and coin, you fill find the following words: "In God We Trust." Let it be known—the entire money supply in the earth belongs to GOD!

Here is what you need to know about your money: Since 1969, the largest denomination of U.S. currency issued is the $100 bill. As larger denomination bills reach the Federal Reserve Bank, they are removed from circulation. Because some discontinued currency is expected to be in the hands of holders for many years, the description of the following denominations continues:

Denomination Presidential Portrait
$1 Washington
$2 Jefferson
$5 Lincoln
$10 Hamilton
$20 Jackson
$50 Grant
$100 Franklin
$500 McKinley
$1,000 Cleveland
$5,000 Madison
$10,000 Chase
$100,000*** Wilson
*** *Denotes for use only in transactions between the Federal Reserve System and the Treasury Department.*

Can you imagine writing out a check for one million dollars? I can.
Here is a fun exercise! Practice writing out the words to the following
denominations listed under "Big Money." Remember, as a man
thinks in his heart so is he. If you can perceive it, you can receive it. If
you think you can, you will. If you think you cannot, you will not!

BIG MONEY

Thousand $1,000.00
Million $1,000,000.00
Billion $1,000,000,000.00
Trillion $1,000,000,000,000.00
Quadrillion $1,000,000,000,000,000.00

Can you imagine yourself with a million dollars, or does the thought
of having a million dollars seem unattainable? How about a billion
dollars? Do you think that a billion dollars is too much money for
one person to have?

I have had people tell me that they can't imagine having a million
dollars because that's too much money. They often say, "besides,
when I die I can't take it with me anyway!"

While the fact remains true that when one dies the money won't
follow them, the truth of the matter is that money left behind can
help your children, your children's children, your church, favorite
charity—the list could go on and on. Whenever God blesses us with
abundance, we are supposed to be a blessing to others.

> "...If you can believe, all things are possible to
> him that believes."
> —Mark 9:23

According to a recent report from the Forbes *World's Richest People*, eight out of the top 10 on the list are Americans.[3] Topping the list is none other than—you guessed it—Bill Gates. Five of the 10 wealthiest people in the world were members of the Walton Family—heirs of the now largest corporation in the world, WalMart®.

Clearly, we can see that attaining billionaire status is possible. In the year 2000, there were 538 billionaires and in 2001, Forbes tracked 497 billionaires, a slight drop from the previous year. You may be wondering how these billionaires got their billions. Having done a little research on these individuals, I found that they were all involved in some type of business.

MONEY CHECK-UP

This exercise will help you to better understand your style of handling money. Place a check mark beside the statement below which best describes you. If more than one description applies to you, place a check mark beside both statements.

1. I...
    A. always buy what I want.
    B. often make spontaneous purchases when I feel I need it.
    C. seldom buy things spontaneously. I carefully think about it first.

2. I...
    A. spend freely on entertainment.
    B. plan for entertainment and pleasurable activities by budgeting for them.
    C. limit entertainment and pleasure in order to save money.

3. I...
    A. usually spend more than I should.
    B. usually spend the right amount and save a portion.
    C. usually spend less than I can afford to spend. I like to save and invest.

4. I...
    A. often buy things I get tired of.
    B. know what I value and spend money only on things which are important.
    C. only spend money on essential items.

5. When purchasing big ticket items (home, car, appliances, etc.) I usually...
   - A. buy without comparison.
   - B. plan, shop and compare prices.
   - C. take a long time and shop conservatively for the best buy.

6. If a financial emergency were to happen today, I...
   - A. would not have the finances to handle the crisis.
   - B. may be able to handle the problem with my savings or get other monies.
   - C. would definitely be able to handle the crisis. I have monies set aside.

7. When purchasing things on credit, I...
   - A. find myself overextended and have difficulty making the payments.
   - B. plan my credit purchases within my budget and make payments.
   - C. never or very seldom make credit purchases.

8. I...
   - A. do not have an idea of my overall monthly expenses.
   - B. am aware of what my monthly expenses are because I plan for them.
   - C. can tell you where and on what I spend every month.

WHAT IS YOUR MONEY-HANDLING STYLE?

If you responded (A) to most of the questions, you have an IMPULSIVE STYLE!

- This style lacks planning
- You spend more money than you have
- You will end up in debt
- This debt will prevent you from reaching personal financial goals
- You are in need of a plan
- A financial plan will help you use money wisely

If you responded (B) to most of the questions, you have a MODERATE STYLE!

- You tend to spend what you earn
- You have a responsible pattern of spending a little less
- You tend to have a long-term financial plan in mind
- You could improve your plan with an accurate budgeting system

If you responded (C) to most of the questions, you have a CONSERVATIVE STYLE!

- You like to be financially secure
- You spend much less than you can afford
- You tend to have a restricting lifestyle
- You use a financial plan
- You maximize your resources for what you enjoy doing most in life

Write out your thoughts on what you just learned about yourself:

_____
_____
_____
_____
_____
_____

What will you do differently?

_____
_____
_____
_____
_____
_____
_____
_____

Biblical Principle: Become a faithful steward over the money you currently have and God will give you more. (See Luke 16:1-12)

CHAPTER 17

WHERE IS THE WEALTH?

In order for you to possess wealth, you must know where it is. Proverbs 13:22 says, *"The wealth of the sinner is laid up for the just."* As I meditated on this scripture, I asked the Lord to show me where the wealth was laid up. The Lord reminded me that prior to entering full-time ministry, my entire adult career was centered on the world of finance. I had a 17-year career as a banker, and I resigned from that career as a vice president of a major bank to follow my call. Immediately after leaving the bank, I was led to study financial planning, intently.

One day as I was sitting in a financial planning class, feeling frustrated knowing I was called to preach, I remember asking the Lord, "What does studying financial planning have to do with me being in full-time ministry?" His response was: "A lot."

The Lord began to show me how those who are wealthy have used His principles, some in a perverted manner, to possess wealth. Most people who have acquired a lot of wealth are liberal givers among themselves and big corporations, primarily for tax purposes. This is how the rich get richer. More is given to those who already have. The perversion comes in because many of the wealthy usually have no regard for the poor, the less fortunate or the Church of the Lord Jesus Christ.

Throughout my banking career, I had numerous opportunities to make acquaintance with men and women of great wealth. I have found that they BELIEVED they were supposed to be rich. The wealthy wicked were FIRMLY PERSUADED that they would have what they say. Many of them set goals to acquire wealth and nothing could separate them from that acquisition. They worked hard, believed their hard work would pay off, and they kept saying and knowing one day they would accumulate wealth.

The wealthy had a constant expectancy to multiply their income and earnings year after year. They put that expectancy in their mouth and spoke it constantly at annual goal-setting meetings, quarterly board meetings, monthly staff meetings, weekly luncheons, daily dinner meetings, etc. They planned to succeed by writing their goals, and executing their plans. In the end, they had good financial success.

Believers need to adopt God's plan for possessing the wealth. Become firmly persuaded like Abraham who,

> "...staggered not at the promise of God through
> unbelief; but was strong in faith, giving glory to God;
> And being fully persuaded that, what he had promised,
> he was able also to perform."
> —Romans 4:20-21

The Amplified Bible Version of this scripture says this of Abraham: *"No unbelief or distrust made him waiver (doubtingly question) concerning the promise of God, but he grew strong and was empowered by faith as he gave praise and glory to God, fully satisfied and assured that God was able and mighty to keep His Word and to do what He had promised."*

You must know that you know that you are supposed to be rich! God promised to make you rich. This promise was made to Abraham and to His seed. In Genesis chapter 17, God appeared to Abram as the almighty all-sufficient God. God told Abram (whose name was changed to Abraham.)

> "And I will make my covenant between me and thee,
> and will multiply thee exceedingly."
> —Genesis 17:2

> "And I will make thee exceeding fruitful, and I will
> make nations of thee, and kings shall come out of thee."
> —Genesis 17:6

> "And I will establish my covenant between me and
> thee and thy seed after thee in their generations for an
> everlasting covenant, to be a God unto thee, and to
> thy seed after thee."
> —Genesis 17:7

If you are a believer, you are Abraham's seed and that promise is still alive today. Galatians 3:21 says: *"And if ye be Christ's, then are ye Abraham's seed, and heirs according to the promise."* God says He keeps covenant for a thousand generations. (Deuteronomy 7:9)

The Lord continued to speak to me about His desire to see His children walk in the fullness of His provisions. He went on to say that the sinners have His wealth and now is the set time for His children to take back what rightfully belongs to them. He began to show me where the wealth of the sinners was stored up.

Again, He showed me how the wealthy have gained their wealth by using His knowledge, His principles and His power. God reminded me that He was the one who created:

REAL ESTATE
STOCK MARKET
COMMODITIES
BOND MARKET
MUTUAL FUNDS
ANNUTIES/INSURANCE

REAL ESTATE

Let me remind you that, as a child of God, land is one of your inheritances.

> "And the Lord appeared unto Abram and said, unto thy seed will I give this land."
> —Genesis 12:7

God says to Abram,

> "For all the land which thou seest, to thee will I give it, and to thy seed for ever."
> —Genesis 13:15

Through this covenant promise, you and I have gained land as our inheritance. Remember, you are Abraham's seed, and heirs according to the promise. God Himself made promises in the following scriptures:

> "And it shall be, when the LORD thy God shall have brought thee into the land which he sware unto thy fathers, to Abraham, to Isaac, and to Jacob, to give thee great and goodly cities, which thou buildedst not, And houses full of all good things, which thou filledst not, and wells digged, which thou diggedst not, vineyards and olive trees, which thou plantedst not; when thou

shalt have eaten and be full;"
—Deuteronomy 6:10, 11

"Hear therefore, O Israel, and observe to do it; that it
may be well with thee, and that ye may increase mightily,
as the Lord God of thy fathers hath promised thee, in
the land that floweth with milk and honey."
—Deuteronomy 6:3

What God promises, He will fulfill. Many who are wealthy in today's society have gotten their wealth through acquiring land. A good example is McDonalds Corporation®. One would think McDonalds® is wealthy solely because of the food they sell. However, the bulk of their wealth comes from owning real estate. Today, McDonalds Corporation® is the largest holding company of real estate in the United States.

How Does One Go About Acquiring Real Estate?
You can purchase property for personal use, commercial use or for rental purposes. Rental property can generate an ongoing income stream, while a seasonal home in which you live earns you no income and is therefore considered a luxury item.

Real Estate Partnerships are created for the purpose of building new structures, generating income from existing properties or money from the appreciation of undeveloped land. Some of the benefits of forming this kind of partnership are that it gives the partners tax shelter and a good stream of income.

Real Estate Investment Trust is the creation of a trust that allows pooled money of many investors to invest in direct ownership of either income property or mortgage loans. These investments also offer tax benefits along with gain of income.

Remember, God said He gives you the power to get wealth

(Deuteronomy 8:18). God gives us His ability and anointing to become wealthy. If He didn't intend for us to possess wealth, He would have never promised to give us the power to get it.

THE STOCK MARKET

When you purchase stock in a company, you are purchasing a portion of that company. You become a stockholder and a partial owner of that corporation because you own the company's stock. In essence, what you have done is loan the company your money in exchange for interest income. In purchasing a company's stock, you have helped them raise money to run their business. Owning stock/equity in a given company is one of the most effective tools used to accumulate wealth.

Let me caution you, however, by telling you there are benefits and risks in owning stock. The benefits are obvious—income. The risks involved center around the volatility of the market (ups and downs, highs and lows) which, in my opinion, is driven by greed and fear. Generally, people sell because of fear of loss and people buy because of the desire to realize gains. This is why there are ups and downs in the market.

Although the stock market poses risks, historically stocks have out-performed conventional investments, such as savings and time deposit accounts. Over the past 10 years, the average range of return on stocks has been somewhere around 10 percent, whereas conventional savings vehicles have only yielded an average rate of return of 4.6 percent.

Two Types Of Stocks Issued by Companies:

Common Stock: Owners of common stock are allowed to exercise control of a company through voting rights. Common stockholders can vote on who will be on the board of directors as well as vote on the dynamics of the company. Voting takes place at annual meetings. If they are unable to physically attend annual board meetings, stockholders can vote by proxy. A proxy vote is an absentee mail-in ballot.

Preferred Stock: Represents an ownership position in the company you invest in. The dividend (your portion of company earnings) is generally predetermined and paid to preferred stockholders before being paid to common stockholders. Unlike the common stockholder, the preferred stockholder does not have voting rights.

Stocks are normally purchased and sold on an exchange market, such as the New York Stock Exchange. If you live in America and listen to a radio or television, you could not have missed our country's love affair with the Stock Market, which is called the Dow Jones Industrial Average.

Throughout the 1990's, the stock market index soared to one record after another. Americans have celebrated the greatest level of prosperity in the history of this great country. Sad to say, many believers were "left behind" as they were oblivious to the accumulation of wealth taking place. Why didn't we participate in this gold rush? I believe it is because we did not have understanding of how to obtain wealth.

While the present market conditions are bleak with stock prices and interest rates at an all time low, investment decisions should be made with expert opinion along with the leading of the Holy Spirit. I'll share more about that shortly. So that you understand the tides of market conditions, I will briefly define two terms we often hear in the news—*Bear Market* and *Bull Market*.

You are probably wondering why we call these markets "bear" and "bull." While no one knows for sure, some market experts have said that these markets got their names simply by how these animals attack their victims. For example, one of the characteristics of the bull is that it drives it's horns up into the air. The bear, on the other hand, swipes it's paws downward upon it's prey. It was also said that, once upon a time, bears and bulls were fierce opponents when they would get into an arena for a fighting match.

Bear Market exists when there is a long-term downward trend in market conditions. The market is considered "bear" if the downward trend lasts more than several months. Another indication that there is a "bear market" stems from falling prices of securities, anywhere from a 15-20 percent downturn.

A bear market signifies that the economy is weak. One can determine that the market is weak by the way businesses are unable to obtain huge profits. During a bear market, consumers tend to spend less, which affects corporate profits, which in return affects the market value of stocks.

Bull Market exists when investors are optimistic about the economy, world events and market conditions. When prices of securities are on the rise, we experience a "bull market." When the market is in the "bull" position, people tend to have more money to spend and they do just that—spend. When we willingly spend money, our economy is strengthened, corporate profits rise, and we usually see a strong demand for the purchase of securities which most investors are unwilling to sell. As a result, we see the prices of securities rise due to this competitive environment.

If you did not participate in the "gold rush of the 90's" where the market was in a 'bull' position, here is an example of what you missed: If you had invested $5,000 in the 30 big industrial stocks that make up the Dow index, your money would have quadrupled to more than $20,000 within less than nine years. If you had invested $10,000 and added, lets say, $50 per month, your total would have increased to almost $65,000 over the same time period. Do you get the picture?

The number of Americans who own stock has increased tremendously over the past decade. Why is there such an increase? It is all due to the unprecedented prosperity within the walls of America. Of course, the level of prosperity can be cyclical, going up and down due to numerous conditions.

The key to realizing good success in the stock market is buying the "right" stock at the right time, and allowing them enough time to ride out the waves—the highs and lows. You must have patience and courage to stay in the market. Some would say, "It's worth the stay." Again, studies continue to show that stocks will outperform other investment vehicles such as certificates of deposits, money markets and even bonds, in the long-run.

A word to the wise! Before you get into the stock market, I strongly encourage you to get wisdom and godly counsel. Find a well-qualified, godly financial consultant, if possible. Most importantly, do not forget to include the all-knowing Counselor—Holy Spirit. He will guide you into all truth. He is the ultimate Counselor.

COMMODITIES/FUTURES

I would like to bring to light a type of investment that is uncommon to many. Commodities are very risky; however, I must make mention of them because God gave an excellent example of commodities/futures in the Bible. A commodity can be agricultural, (e.g., gas, oil, cattle, soybeans, pork bellies, and molasses), or non-agricultural (e.g., wood, silver, gold, or other financial futures such as treasury bills and/ or treasury notes).

Commodity traders buy and sell contracts based on speculation of price increase and decrease. In other words, they know beforehand whether the price of a commodity will go up or go down. This type of investment could give a high rate of return; however, the risk is unlimited. One's loss can far exceed one's investment. Let's look at a Biblical example of how this works.

I draw your attention to the book of Genesis, Chapter 41 where Pharaoh had a dream and Joseph (a Hebrew servant) interpreted Pharaoh's dream. The dream interpretation was that of a modern day commodity/future contract. Joseph, with the help of Holy Spirit, interpreted the dream. Joseph gathered up all the food over the seven years of plenty.

> "Behold there come seven years of great plenty
> throughout all the land of Egypt. And there shall
> arise after them seven years of famine; and all the
> plenty shall be forgotten in the land of Egypt; and
> the famine shall consume the land."
> —Genesis 41:29-30

> "And the seven years of dearth (famine) began to
> come, according as Joseph had said: and the dearth
> (famine) was in all the lands; but in all the land of
> Egypt there was bread."
> —Genesis 41:54

> "And when all the land of Egypt was famished, the
> people cried to Pharaoh for bread: and Pharaoh
> said unto all the Egyptians, go unto Joseph; what he
> saith to you, do. And the famine was over all the face
> of the earth: and Joseph opened all the storehouses,
> and sold unto the Egyptians; and the famine waxed
> sore in the land of Egypt. And all the countries came
> into Egypt to Joseph for to buy corn; because that the
> famine was so sore in all lands."
> —Genesis 41:55-57

Egypt became rich because the wisdom of God was revealed through a man of God. Joseph knew beforehand that there would be a famine and there would be a need to store up food. This is an example of commodities/futures where you know beforehand whether a commodity will go up or go down.   Here again, a child of God had the wisdom of God and that wisdom brought him and his people wealth.

BOND MARKET

"For the Lord thy God blesseth thee, as He promised thee: and thou shalt lend unto many nations, but thou shalt not borrow; and thou shall reign over many nations, but they shall not reign over thee."
—Deuteronomy 15:6

HOW DO YOU LEND TO NATIONS?

How do you lend to nations? The answer is by purchasing bonds. When you purchase bonds, you are loaning money to the entity that you are purchasing the bonds from. For example, if you own U.S. savings bonds, you have loaned the U.S. money, which they in turn use to fund and assist nations throughout the world.

Clearly, bonds represent an investor's loan to the issuing party. The entity issuing the bond is called the borrower. The borrower promises to repay the loan and pay interest to the lender for a specified time. Corporations issue bonds to raise money for company's expenses. Although the bondholder does not have ownership in said company, bondholders are paid before common and preferred stockholders, should a company file bankrupt or go out of business.

There are seven types of bonds to choose from, including: U.S. government securities, municipal bonds, corporate bonds, mortgage and asset-backed securities, federal agency securities and foreign government bonds. The government owes over $5 trillion dollars in bonds. Who does the government owe this money to? These monies are owed to those who invest in government bonds. Have you been lending to nations? It is not too late to get started.

WHY INVEST IN BONDS?

It is a good idea for investors to maintain a diversified investment portfolio consisting of bonds, stocks, precious metals and cash. The percentages should vary, depending upon individual circumstances and objectives. Because bonds generally have a predictable income stream, many people invest in them to preserve and to increase their capital.

Bonds are a good way to help achieve your financial objectives. A financial representative can help explain the numerous investment options available to help you reach your objectives.

MUTUAL FUNDS

A mutual fund comes from corporations that pool large sums of money, ranging from one million to several billions of dollars, from millions of individual investors, just like you, who wish to save or make money. An individual or a team of professional money managers invests the pooled money into stocks, bonds, or other securities.

The combined holdings of a mutual fund are known as the fund's portfolio. An individual who owns shares in a mutual fund may invest as little as $25-$50, or as much as $2,500 or more. You don't have to be rich to have your money working for you.

By investing money into a mutual fund, your money is spread out and diversified among hundreds of stocks, bonds, or other securities; therefore, minimizing risk. Through the purchase of mutual funds, you do not need to buy bonds and stocks directly and you are not limited to the volatile performance of owning merely one or two stocks.

In addition to this, you pay minimal fees, often less than one percent of your investment (per year), while earning money with the expertise of the mutual fund managers. Studies have shown that when you invest in mutual funds, you will make more money than you would by leaving the funds in a bank account where you may actually lose money and spending power.

BENEFITS OF MUTUAL FUNDS

Anyone, no matter what their age or income, should and can invest in mutual funds! Mutual funds are an easy, inexpensive way for an individual to capture the money that is to be made from stocks and bonds, without buying them directly.

The good thing about this type of investment is that an investor does not even have to have expert knowledge of stocks and bonds, nor does he have to pay high commission fees in order to make money with minimal risk. Investing in mutual funds is a good way to save money for the short-term and long-term future, such as for college, retirement, a car, a home, a vacation and more.

MUTUAL FUND OBJECTIVES

The goal of a mutual fund is to provide an efficient way for an individual to make money. There are several thousand mutual funds, with different investment strategies and goals to choose from. Choosing one can be overwhelming, although it doesn't have to be. Different mutual funds have different risks, based on factors such as the fund's goals, the fund's manager, and investment styles. Money from a mutual fund is made when the stocks, bonds, or other securities increase in value (a capital gain), issue dividends or make interest payments.

Capital gains, income, and/or dividend payments (share of profit paid to a stockholder) best serve the young investor when reinvested. Most retirees often seek income from dividend distributions to supplement their income. With reinvestment of dividends and capital gains distributions, your money increases at an even greater rate.

Investing in a mutual fund is a long-term commitment, generally a minimum of three to five years. Before investing in a mutual fund, ask for its current prospectus. The prospectus provides important information about a fund's investment objectives, policies, procedures, services, and fees. Read it carefully before you invest. Remember, the past performance of a mutual fund is not a guarantee of future fund performance.

ANNUITIES

Annuities are long-term, tax-deferred investments that offer many options to help meet today's financial needs. Fixed annuities offer stability of principal and interest rates guaranteed for up to ten years. Variable annuities may offer the opportunity for above market rates of return, but your investment value may fluctuate on a daily basis.

When you buy an annuity, the insurance company invests your money according to the terms of your annuity contract or policy. Annuities are a product of the insurance industry and are the exclusive obligation of the issuing company. You should investigate the financial soundness of any insurance company before you invest in their products. Most insurance company's financial ratings are available at most public libraries.

UNDERSTANDING INVESTMENT RISKS

As you begin to invest, it is important to understand the investment options available and the risks and rewards associated with each opportunity before investing. Generally speaking, the more risk you are willing to take, the greater your rewards may be. You set the level of risk by your comfort with risk; do not exceed your limit no matter what wonderful promises you hear.

For short-term investments, you probably don't want to take much risk. For longer-term investments, you may want to consider a more aggressive investment that may move upward over time. Become an educated investor. Find a godly, professional financial consultant who can further assist you in achieving your investment goals.

CHAPTER 18
THE IMPORTANCE OF BUDGETING

Every household should have a budget/spending plan so that impulses to spend can be controlled. A budget will show you a picture of where your money is going. If you are completing a budget for the first time, you will be surprised to find how much money you waste on liabilities. Liabilities are things that you purchase that do not earn you money, (e.g., excessive shoes, clothes, jewelry, gadgets, etc.)

One of the things you should condition yourself to do is to stop buying liabilities (things that take money out of your hands without any return on your investment) and start buying assets—things, which will make you money. Each time you make a purchase, ask yourself, "will this purchase make money or create a liability?" Keep in mind that you do need necessities such as food, clothing, and shelter. Still, ask yourself, "How much do I really need? Am I spending too much on these items?"

I once read about a family whose finances were "messed up," due to indebtedness. The husband was overseeing the finances at that time. It was suggested that the wife would take on that responsibility for a certain time period, just to see what happens. When the wife started to handle the finances, she immediately cut out all spending. The only thing they purchased were things that were absolutely necessary. There was no more dining out; everyone had to take their lunch, and they entertained themselves by doing things which were free. Six months went by and their debt load was drastically reduced.

If you are going to see change in your financial outlook, you must change the way you handle money. A definition of insanity is doing the same things over and over again, expecting different results. In order to get different results, you have to change what you are doing. The first step in this change process is creating a budget.

You are encouraged to complete annual as well as monthly budgets. Keep in mind, budgets or spending plans are always subject to change. The purpose of the budget is to track and control where your money goes. It is a good idea to monitor your progress weekly, and make adjustments if needed. The goal of budgeting is to cut expenses and increase your month-end surplus, resulting in extra cash.

DEVELOPING A MONEY SPENDING PLAN

"...Write the vision, and make it plain upon tables,
that he may run that readeth it."
—Habakkuk 2:2

It is godly wisdom to have a plan for everything you do—including spending money. Planning how to spend your paycheck will help control the impulses to spend. Many people have a problem with budgets. If you are one of them, let's find out why so you can overcome the obstacles preventing you from completing and sticking to a budget. This is a critical step as you move on to a position of wealth.

Overcoming Budgetary Obstacles

List Five Reasons Why You Cannot Complete a Budget.

1._____

_____

2._____

_____

3._____

_____

4._____

_____

5._____

_____

How Do You Plan to Overcome These Obstacles?

1._____

_____

2._____

_____

3._____

_____

4._____

_____

5._____

_____

HOW TO PREPARE A BUDGET

Budgets should be prepared monthly as well as annually. The budget will identify your income and outflow of cash.

Establish your goal. The primary goal of most budgets is to track and control where your money is going. Budgets are also used to cut expenses and increase your month-end surplus.

Identify all income. It is important to know exactly how much income you have at your disposal.

Maintain records! This can be challenging; however, this is a crucial step in the budget preparation process. It is important that you keep an accurate record of every penny you spend. Be sure to keep receipts and log all checkbook activity.

Reconcile records on a monthly basis. Cross-reference bank statements. Confirm that all deposits were applied accordingly and that all checks and debits were subtracted for the correct amount. Do the same for all monthly statements—mortgage statements, credit card statements, etc.

It is a good idea to look at your progress often. Measure your progress towards your initial goals. Perhaps changes should be made to alter your initial plan. Keep in mind, budgets are a working document and therefore require adjustments from time to time.

On the following pages are sample categories of expenses which may appear on a monthly budget.

LET'S GET STARTED!

BUDGET/SPENDING PLAN WORKSHEET

Name/Household:_____

Month/Year :_____

Categories/Items	Monthly Payment	Annual Payment
Gross Monthly Income	$_____	$_____
Subtract Tithes (10%)	$_____	$_____
Federal Taxes	$_____	$_____
State Taxes	$_____	$_____
Soc. Security	$_____	$_____
Insurance	$_____	$_____
Offering	$_____	$_____
Savings/Invest	$_____	$_____
Other Deductions	$_____	$_____
Total Monthly Deductions	$_____	$_____
Monthly Income - Deductions = Net Income Available	$_____	$_____

Housing Expenses

	Monthly Payment	Annual Payment
Rent or Mortgage Payment	$_____	$_____
Second Mortgage	$_____	$_____
Real Estate Taxes (1/12)	$_____	$_____
Rental/Homeowners Insurance	$_____	$_____
Other Housing Expenses	$_____	$_____
Total Housing Expenses	$_____	$_____
Total This Page	$_____	$_____

BUDGET/SPENDING PLAN WORKSHEET — PAGE 2

Categories/Items	Monthly Payment	Annual Payment
Utilities		
Water	$_____	$_____
Gas	$_____	$_____
Electric	$_____	$_____
Telephone	$_____	$_____
Cellular Phone	$_____	$_____
Cable/Satellite	$_____	$_____
Total Utilities	$_____	$_____
Food		
Groceries	$_____	$_____
Lunch	$_____	$_____
Dining Out	$_____	$_____
Total Food Consumption	$_____	$_____
Clothing		
Clothing & Shoes	$_____	$_____
Hosiery	$_____	$_____
Laundry/Cleaners	$_____	$_____
Jewelry & Accessories	$_____	$_____
Outerwear	$_____	$_____
Total Clothing	$_____	$_____
Personal Care		
Hair and Nails	$_____	$_____
Cosmetics & Toiletries	$_____	$_____
Child Care	$_____	$_____
Personal Shopper	$_____	$_____
Total Personal Care	$_____	$_____
Total This Page	$_____	$_____

BUDGET/SPENDING PLAN WORKSHEET — PAGE 3

Categories/Items	Monthly Payment	Annual Payment
Transportation		
Auto Note(s)	$_____	$_____
Insurance	$_____	$_____
Maintenance/Repairs	$_____	$_____
Gas	$_____	$_____
Public Transportation	$_____	$_____
Total Transportation	$_____	$_____
Entertainment		
Movies/ Music	$_____	$_____
Concerts/Plays	$_____	$_____
Sporting Events/Activities	$_____	$_____
Total Entertainment	$_____	$_____
Miscellaneous		
Books/Magazines/Newspapers	$_____	$_____
Vacations	$_____	$_____
Credit Card(s)	$_____	$_____
Retirement/College funding	$_____	$_____
Bank fees	$_____	$_____
Private School Tuition	$_____	$_____
Other	$_____	$_____
Total Miscellaneous	$_____	$_____
Total This Page	$_____	$_____
Total Page 1	$_____	$_____
Total Page 2	$_____	$_____
Total Page 3	$_____	$_____
Grand Total	$_____	$_____

Net Income Available - Grand Total =   Surplus   or   Deficit
                                         Extra   or   Not Enough

CHAPTER 19
FINANCIAL PLANNING

"...Write the vision, and make it plain upon tables,
that he may run that readeth it."
—Habakkuk 2:2

Having a financial plan in place is very essential to accumulating wealth. Perhaps you are not at a point where you need a financial planner. If you do not have much in earnings, you probably don't need a planner. However, you need to plan in order to arrive at the point of receiving the wealth God has in store for you.

As we have already discussed, you should start your planning with a budget, or perhaps a "money spending plan" sounds better. I have come to realize most people despise the "B" word—budget—because they feel having a budget restricts their spending habits.

To not plan can be detrimental to your financial state of being. Before you spend, you should know how much you are able to spend. Oftentimes, we spend what we don't have and then we resort to using credit. I will speak about that false prosperity (living on credit) in a later chapter.

HOW FINANCIAL PLANNERS CAN HELP

A well-trained planner can sit down with you and your family and help you make essential savings and investment decisions. This plan should cover the household's financial goals, including: budget, insurance, tolerance for risk, asset allocation, retirement plan, and a review of an estate plan. Such detailed planning is unlikely to be met by brokers and agents who are more interested in commissions on financial products they sell.

As mentioned before, not everyone needs a professional planner. Some people choose to do their own planning themselves. On the other hand, many families apparently believe they are candidates for professional help.

A survey done by Harris Interactive Inc., for the American Institute of Certified Public Accountants found that the majority of respondents say they are spending more time thinking about their finances. However, less than a third are confident they can manage money as well as they could with the help of a financial planner.

When I refer to a financial planner, I am describing someone with the expertise to produce a comprehensive financial plan for an individual's household. A financial planner should have a broad knowledge of areas such as tax planning, investments, and estate law, but they are unlikely to be the financial professional you require in these individual areas. Rather, the financial planner can help to coordinate your financial planning with your accountant, insurance agent, investment professional, and estate lawyer. The broad expertise that a professional financial planner possesses will help ensure that your financial goals are met and that all areas of your financial life are reviewed.

One thing to understand is that planners, of course, cost money.

Some charge flat fees for specified services. Others charge hourly rates. Still others work on commissions they earn from products they sell to you. You may ask the question, "Is one method better than the other?" Whatever your choice, make sure the form of payment is disclosed fully.

CHOOSING A FINANCIAL PLANNER

In the United States, there are between 200,000 and 300,000 individuals who call themselves "Financial Planners." When selecting a financial planner, I suggest that you look for a Christian, professional Certified Financial Planner who is highly qualified. Among the many professional designations planners might have, some are Certified Financial Planner, Chartered Financial Consultant or Personal Financial Specialist. All of these professionals receive such designations after completion of extensive training courses and exams.

Hiring a planner will help you avoid expensive financial mistakes that could seriously damage your financial health. It would not be difficult for most financial planners to find serious gaps in most household finances—gaps that are easily worth the cost of the planner's services.

Even individuals with expert knowledge in one financial field, such as investments, can overlook areas such as insurance or estate planning. With today's fast- paced schedules, few people have the time, desire, or expertise to do a complete comprehensive financial plan on their own.

The first step in looking for a financial planner is to limit your search to someone who is certified in Financial Planning. The second step is to seek recommendations from people that you respect. Ask for names of financial planners and interview these planners.

Your aim is to find someone who meets your needs and who will look after your interests. A problem that exists in selecting financial professionals is that what is in your best interest may fall a distant second to what is in their interest of making a profit.

Next, you need to find out how the financial planner receives their compensation, and what it will cost you annually. Compensation for financial planners falls into two broad types: *fee-only or fee-based.*

Fee-Only: Planners typically charge by the hour to evaluate your financial situation, and to make specific recommendations. They provide comprehensive investment management, which includes: investment advice; financial planning; insurance; retirement planning; college planning; business planning; estate and tax planning; and asset protection planning. They typically do not receive any commissions from your investments and insurance products you purchase.

Fee-Based: They typically charge a fee for financial advice and receive commissions on the investment and insurance products they recommend. Fee-based planners provide the same comprehensive investment management services that fee-only planners provide.

It is important that you choose the one that is right for you. Everyone's financial picture is different, thus the type of advisor you use will vary from fee-based to fee-only. While some give the nod automatically to fee-only financial planners, it will depend on your particular circumstances as to which one will be best for you.

Given this information on financial planners, it is clear that your gaining knowledge is very important. While many households will spend a great deal of time shopping for an automobile, the decision of whom to trust with their wealth is often made without much thought.

HOW TO INVEST FOR RETIREMENT

Did you know you became a retirement saver the day you collected your first paycheck? The evidence was right there on the stub, labeled "FICA." Unfortunately, social security by itself won't pay for the good life you'd like—never has, never will. That is why you should put your trust in God and not in your savings and investments.

To afford that condominium on the golf course some day, or even that one-bedroom apartment in leisure world, you have to accumulate and preserve your wealth by following God's pathway. Saving and investing is one way to accumulate wealth. But you knew that, right? No wonder retirement is most often the goal people have in mind for investment plans.

Maybe retirement isn't your top-priority goal right now. Maybe you have other financial commitments to deal with first. Keeping your eye on that far horizon will help you take heed when the immediate investment climate looks bleak and you're tempted to spend instead of save.

SETTING FINANCIAL GOALS

Setting a goal serves another purpose: With a concrete objective in mind, you can undertake the essential task of estimating what your financial goal will cost. If your goal is affording a comfortable retirement, it's not that difficult to figure out that number.

A good rule of thumb is to figure that you will need somewhere around 70 to 100 percent of your pre-retirement income to live comfortably once you retire. Other questions to consider: What kind of lifestyle do you plan to live—the life of a world traveler, a "happy homebody," or perhaps even somewhere in between?

You also want to consider whether you will stay in the home you are currently living in or move to some place less or more expensive. Your answers to questions like these will determine your living expenses and how much you will need to travel, shop, and enjoy your life. Of course, this is all after you have given your tithes and offerings.

INCOME YOU CAN COUNT ON?

The Social Security Administration will provide you with a personalized benefits estimate. This statement will show you how much you have paid into social security year-to-date. You can obtain this information by calling 1 800-772-1213. (This phone number may change; check your local directory.)

In addition, if you have a traditional pension plan at work, the plan administrator can tell you what to expect under any number of options you might choose. Subtract the amount of social security and pension benefits you will receive from the amount you estimate you will need in the first year of retirement. The difference between the two is the estimated amount you will need from other sources to cover each year of retirement. Supplemental sources may include investments you've already made, such as IRA accounts and 401(k) retirement-plan accounts you may have participated in.

SAVING FOR COLLEGE

Every success is first a prayer success. I suggest that you begin to pray for God's favor to go before you and your children so that they can obtain fully-paid scholarships to the universities of their choice. One of my friends recently received an answer to prayer when her son, a high school graduate, received a full academic scholarship to a choice university. Prayer works!

Another point to consider is developing a savings plan to pay college tuition. Parents of newborns have all heard variations of this eye-opening fact. Four years of tuition at a public college should cost about $96,000 in 18 years. If you were to put $5 a day into a cookie jar for each of those 18 years, you would have only saved a little more than one-third of that sum.

Even if you put that $5 a day into a savings account that earns four percent, you would still have only half the necessary funds. That said, it is imperative that you start to save for your child's college education, or for any other goal that is seven or more years away. You still have time on your side.

First, estimate the total cost of your child's future college education. Annual in-state tuition for a public school now averages about $4,000 - $10,000. The cost increases up to threefold for private and topnotch institutions of higher learning.

If you factor in five percent a year for college-cost inflation, 10 years from now a single year at a public college could cost about $16,300 -- and $53,800 at a private school. For four years, that would total about $65,000 and $215,200, respectively. I know this may sound alarming. Don't be alarmed. Put your faith in God. He will open doors and lead you in His infinite wisdom to bring your desire to educate your child to pass.

> "The desire of the righteous shall be granted."
> —Proverbs 10:24

You should also consider what kind of investment account could help maximize your earnings. If you will have a child in college when you are 59-1/2 years old, a Roth IRA may be suitable because all of your withdrawals will be tax-free (provided you've had the account for at least five years). These laws are subject to change.

How you invest is essential to knowing how much money you will have available at the time your child goes to college. A financial planner or your banker can give you additional insight on how to save and invest for college.

Chapter 20
DEALING WITH BANKRUPTCY

Is Bankruptcy Scriptural?

"The wicked borrow and pay not again [for they may be unable], but the uncompromisingly righteous deal kindly and give [for they are able]."
                                        —Psalm 37:21 AMP

That's what God's Word says. If you borrow and do not pay it back, He said you are wicked; therefore we can see that bankruptcy is a moral issue one has to consider.

Don't be condemned if you have or are contemplating filing bankruptcy. Learn from your mistakes, repent, and do not allow yourself to get into a position of filing bankruptcy, going forward.

Many people consider bankruptcy to be an option to get out of debt. Unfortunately, many who file for bankruptcy end up repeating the process simply because they put a bandage on their problem instead of correcting the problem of living above their means. While some people see filing for bankruptcy as a way of getting a fresh start, having been relieved of certain debt, consider this:

A bankruptcy status stays on your credit report for at least 10 years, making it very difficult to buy a home, get life insurance, or sometimes even get a job. When I was a banker who made loans, I saw first hand the mental anguish of those who suffered from the difficulty of purchasing a home or even a car.

While bankruptcy is looked upon as the "Big Fix," there are repercussions that follow bankruptcies. The reason second-time bankruptcies are on the rise is because most of the spending habits of those filing bankrupt remain the same, and when things get tight, subconsciously they know there is a way of escape.

The initial intent for allowing one to file bankruptcy stemmed from allowing those individuals/companies who experienced catastrophe to have relief from financial demise. Most people confuse the difference between catastrophe and self-indulgence, due to an "I've got to have it now, microwave mentality." Become disciplined with spending and you will not have to go this route.

TYPES OF PERSONAL BANKRUPTCY

There are two types of personal bankruptcy. Both are filed in a Federal Bankruptcy Court. There are fees involved with filing. There is a blanket fee of approximately $160, a $130 filing fee plus an administrative fee ranging from $30-$40. Remember, these fees may vary.

Chapter 7
Most people file Chapter 7 because it allows for elimination of most consumer debt, such as medical bills and credit cards. This type of bankruptcy, however, requires you to sell your assets. The only assets one may be allowed to keep is the primary residence, first car, and some home furnishings.

If you have multiple cars, vacation homes, and other luxury items, these items will be sold and the proceeds will be turned over to your creditors. Filing Chapter 7 will immediately stop collection efforts by your creditors. At this point, the creditor cannot garnish your paycheck, foreclose your property, repossess your vehicle, or go after your assets.

Chapter 13

With Chapter 13 filing, a court appointed official will establish a repayment plan which allows you to pay off defaulted debt over a five-year period. You do not have to surrender and liquidate your assets in this case, provided you have steady income which allows you to make some type of monthly payment.

You will find that those who are behind in their mortgage payments and do not want their property foreclosed tend to file chapter 13. After all payments are made under an established plan, you will receive a discharge of your debt.

In both instances, personal bankruptcy does not relieve an individual of paying bills associated with the government such as taxes, child support, or student loans. Remember, both filings will appear on your credit report for at least 10 years.

EXCESSIVE DEBT + MARRIAGE = PROBLEMS

Studies show that the number one cause for divorce is money problems. Debt plus marriage equals trouble. I would advise anyone who is considering getting married to get your debt under control before tying the knot. Credit reports are increasingly becoming a part of marriage counseling sessions and rightfully so. It is a God idea to be honest with your spouse and/or your potential spouse about how you handle money.

Married couples as well as singles get into debt by allowing societal pressures to direct the way they spend. This results in living beyond the means provided in an effort to keep up with the "Joneses." Who are the Joneses, anyway? Besides, do they have a heaven to put you in? Why then, do we allow ourselves to get into debt in order to impress those around us?

Today, almost half of those seeking consumer credit counseling are married couples. I believe a part of the reason why this happens is due to a lack of trust in the area of money. Many married couples maintain separate lives on the money front. One has no idea how much money the other makes or spends. They have secret, separate accounts, "just in case."

I have heard older women advise younger women to "always have a rainy day fund on the side just in case he leaves you." We enter marriages planning to fail. God said,

> "Therefore shall a man leave his father and his mother, and shall cleave unto his wife: and they shall be one flesh."
>
> —Genesis 2:24

We should enter the marriage union with a plan to succeed and not allow bad decisions on handling finances to dismantle our marriages.

The following are tactics you may use to get debt out of your marriage:

Begin to put your finances together. Oftentimes in a marriage, you will find one spouse is a miser while the other is a spender. This is good because you complete each other and bring balance to the marriage. You make the call on who will oversee the finances.

The key is communicating with each other about all expenditures so that you can remain on track. Schedule a time to meet weekly or bi-weekly to discuss and update each other on your finances.

Make decisions together.

> "Do two walk together except they make an
> appointment and have agreed?"
> —Amos 3:3 AMP

Make it a point to understand that you and your partner's money styles were shaped by an accumulation of life experiences. Just because your partner is different from you when it comes to money, that does not mean he or she is wrong. The key is for the two of you to come into agreement about your financial goals.

CHAPTER 21
THERE IS LIFE AFTER DEBT

"Nowadays people can be divided into three classes: the haves, the have-nots and the have-not-paid-for-what-they-haves."
—Earl Wilson, American Journalist

I am a living witness that there is life after debt. When I was a junior attending Howard University, I was walking around with 12 credit cards—I had gas cards, Visas, Mastercards, Sears, Woodward and Lothrop, Garfinkel's—you name it, I had it. Credit and more credit.

Many creditors prey on college students who are about to graduate because the expectation is that the graduate will get a good job and have the ability to repay the debt. Although my mother warned me about getting those cards, I was just like a kid being warned not to touch the hot surface on the stove. I would tell my Mom, "Okay Mommy, I know, don't use the cards because I will get in debt."

Basically I gave my mother lip service. In my mind, I would say— "She's just old. She's just over cautious." Of course I went about charging up a storm. I remember purchasing a wonderful leather dress for roughly $700. I was 20 years old! My rationale was, it's my 20th birthday and I deserve it. After all, nothing is too good for me.

By the time I paid off or should I say, settled that account, the cost of that $700 dress had doubled. I have heard people say that the best teacher is experience. Boy, were they wrong! The best teacher is wisdom by the Holy Spirit.

Being in debt over my head was not a good experience. This caused such pain and agony. Not to mention my parents saying, "Your ears can't hear, your behind will feel it." What my parents were saying was—"I told you so!"

I remember graduating from Howard University with a good job offer; however, I was in debt. When I got paid, all my money was going to the creditors. I was working for Exxon, Visa, Mastercard, Sears, and all the people I owed. I was under obligation to, enslaved and indebted to them. But thanks be unto God! There is life after debt.

Eventually, a way of escape was made. The accounts were paid off; however, I was left with bad credit. I quickly learned that truly a good name is more precious than expensive ointment. (Ecclesiastes 7:1) I now understand the importance of having good credit. I am also fully aware of the proper usage of money and credit.

Today, it appears that so many people are looking to get rich quick. Because we live in a "microwave" society, we want what we want when we want it. We have a mentality that says credit is a way of life in America.

Many people have embraced the credit culture and are living on false prosperity. False prosperity is "assumed" wealth rather than earned wealth. Many people appear to be wealthy. They have fine clothes, nice jewelry, expensive furs and fully loaded cars. They have accumulated possessions. However, the reality is they are living on credit or assumed wealth.

I know the comment I am about to make is a stinger; however, it is truth. There are many people wearing clothes, driving cars and living in homes belonging to banks, finance and mortgage companies. When asked the question, "Do you own your own home?" The person purchasing a home will respond, "Yes."

However, the truth is that the bank or the mortgage company owns the home. You are simply paying towards owning that home. You become owner of the home when the loan is paid in full and you have a deed which is free and clear of any liens. How do I know this? If you miss successive auto or mortgage payments, you will quickly find out that you are not the owner of that property. Instead, the true owners of the property will repossess and foreclose what you thought was your car or your house.

It does not help that in today's society it is very easy to become overloaded with debt, because creditors have made the process for acquiring credit fairly easy. For example, I am bombarded, weekly, with credit card companies making offers to obtain credit, transfer balances and receive a low introductory rate.

Before acquiring credit, you should give much thought to credit's consequences by asking yourself: "How will I repay this debt?" Should I buy what I cannot afford? Can I exercise delayed gratification today to have a more prosperous tomorrow?

I believe we need to get back to basics. Most people who have amassed wealth did so by using their God-given gifts and talents to work, save their earnings, make wise investments, and manage their money properly.

We cannot arrive at our wealthy place if we are in debt. The Bible equates being in debt with being in bondage. The borrower is servant to the lender. (Proverbs 22:7) It is time for the Body of Christ to get out of debt. The first step in doing so is acknowledging the problem.

Identify and take authority over the spirit of debt. We must get in control of over-spending and hyper-consumption. Whenever you are faced with a problem, it is important that you take ownership and look for ways to solve the problem.

If you are in debt, you do not have to stay there. If you are headed for debt disaster, turn around and go the other way. Stop doing whatever you are doing to increase debt. As I said earlier, if you keep doing the same thing, you will continue to get the same results.

The National Foundation for Credit Counseling and other experts suggest asking yourself the following questions:

- Are you borrowing to pay for items that you used to buy with cash?

- Are you taking out new loans before paying off previous loans?

- Are monthly installment bills, besides rent or mortgage, more than 15 percent of your take-home pay?

- Are creditors threatening to repossess your car, home, credit cards, or to take other legal action?

- Are your expenses growing faster than your income?

- Do you dip into savings to pay regular bills?

- Is your savings reserve less than three months of your take-home pay?

- Are you approaching the limits of all your credit lines?

- Do you use savings to pay off old bills?

- Are you usually late in paying bills?

- Do you make only minimum payments each month?

- Do you find it hard to save at least 10 percent of your take-home pay?

- Are you borrowing from one lender to pay another?

- Do you regularly overdraw your checking account?

- Do lenders require a friend or relative to co-sign your loans?

- Are you unable to say how much money you owe?

- Are you fighting with your spouse or family members over money?

- Are you living from "paycheck to paycheck?"

These are warning signs that you are piling up too much debt. Before you acquire credit, before you spend, ask yourself these questions: "Is this good or bad debt? Will this purchase earn or cost me money?"

It is easy to differentiate what is good versus bad debt. Good debt will produce income or cash flow, while bad debt takes away from your cash flow. For example, purchasing an apartment building or rental property will produce revenue. This would be considered good debt.

In general, mortgage debt is good debt. Yes, it is borrowed money; however, you are at a tax advantage since you are allowed to write off the interest on appreciating assets. Some would argue that mortgages are bad because a mortgage is "a death grip" in terms of the length of time to pay off and the cost associated with having a mortgage.

Some would further argue that although a home is an appreciating asset, you are spending money on up-keep, property taxes and the mere fact that the home you live in does not produce monthly cash flow. Nevertheless, we all need shelter. Ideally, I would rather live in a home that I own fully without mortgage payments.

I believe that parents, along with our education system, should provide financial education for our children so that they won't grow up to be adults lacking financial understanding. There is so much information available for this and every topic of your interest. However, we must take time to read and research this all-important topic of financial success.

TAKE CONTROL OF YOUR SPENDING HABITS

Love not the world neither the things that are in the world. This is what gets us into debt: lust of the flesh and lust of the eyes and the pride of life. (See 1 John 2:15-16).

- Create a budget you are comfortable with and stick with it.

- Do not use a credit card if you cannot pay it off as soon as the bill comes in the mail.

- Avoid the impulse to buy just because something is on sale.

- Always wait a day before deciding to make large purchases.

- Do not buy things you did not plan to buy.

- Get rid of mail-order catalogs.

- Stay away from malls and shopping strips.

- Avoid large car, house, and apartment payments.

- Make a decision to spend less than you make.

- Select one major credit card with the lowest annual interest rate, and cut up all others.

- Become aggressive in paying down bad debt.

"He who has no rule over his own spirit is like a city that is broken down and without walls."
                                                    —Proverbs 25:28

HOW TO BREAK OUT OF DEBT

"The rich ruleth over the poor, and the borrower is servant to the lender."
                                                    —Proverbs 22:7

God never intended for His children to be in debt. God want His children to be debt free so that they can owe no man anything, but to love one another. (Romans 13:8)

Paying high interest on loans is your enemy.

"The thief comes not, but for to steal, and to kill, and to destroy."
                                                    —John 10:10

For this and many other reasons, we should flee from debt. As a believer, you have the answer to all questions on the inside of you. Seek the Lord for His direction on getting you out of debt. He will show you. I am debt free today because I sought God for His counsel. Seek God; He will show you things to do in the natural to eliminate your debt. Once you get out, don't go back!

Do not allow the enemy to steal your joy, kill your spirit, and destroy your soul through the entanglement of debt. Being head over-heels in debt is an outflow of so many social problems—including depression, relational problems and marital problems—which sometimes lead to divorce.

Oftentimes, we want a quick fix from God. You know. We often ask for "supernatural debt cancellation." I think it is great to believe God to do the impossible! In fact, in the book of Nehemiah chapter 5 verse 11, God talks about debt cancellation. God can suddenly have your debt eliminated. Most of us, however, would get right back into debt.

For that reason, God uses processes to eliminate ugly situations in our lives. Everything we do in life is done through a process. It took a gradual process for you to get into debt and it will take a process of learning to be disciplined in handling money to get out of debt. You did not get into debt overnight, did you? Until your debt cancellation miracle comes from God, you should take steps to reduce your debt.

Find out what your lifestyle costs. You cannot figure out how to pay down any debt without first figuring out your expenses. Figure out what you are spending.

Spend less than you make. It's a simple choice.

Make more than you spend. The choice is yours. You are probably spending more than you make. Now you must figure out what you're going to stop buying, or what you're going to sell. For example, you could unload a second car or home to cut down on expenses.

Dine in. Prepare a healthy salad, or make pancakes or waffles and scrambled eggs for dinner. It could be a nice change. Food is one of the biggest holes in many family budgets.

Quit trying to be a super dresser and a fashion plate! Clothes don't make the person. You can save a ton of money if you stop trying to dress the part of the movie stars in designer clothing. Ask yourself, "how many outfits can I wear at one time?"

Live substantially below your income. Sacrifice now so you can have financial peace later.

Don't think refinancing your mortgage or getting a home equity loan eliminates debt. You are simply rolling over and deferring the debt.

Pay more than the minimum monthly payment on your credit card debt.

Send in your payment as soon as the bill arrives. In doing so, you could avoid finance charges by paying the balance.

Analyze your monthly statement for accuracy. You will find the minimum monthly payment in many instances does not cover the finance charges being applied. That's why it takes forever to pay off revolving credit.

Pass on offers to skip a payment. This deferred payment is just like making another purchase.

If possible, consolidate credit cards to one low interest card. You will be better able to keep track and make timely payments.

Read the fine print on the company's ability to increase interest rate at will.

Attack your bills. Make a list of all outstanding balances and their minimum monthly payments; then pay an extra $20, $30, or $40 per month towards one bill. Once that bill is paid, do the same for the next bill until all revolving debt is paid off.

Pay off every card that charges you the most to keep a balance. The quicker you cut down on high-rate debt, the more money you'll save in the long run.

Keep paying the extra dollars even though the balances and the minimum monthly payments will drop. The more you pay, the faster you will see debt disappear.

Stop using plastic. Pay cash. If you are unable to pay cash for it, more than likely you don't need it.

Pay all your bills on time. Late payments cost $25-45. When you are late in making payments, credit card companies can hike your interest rate significantly.

Tell the truth. Admit you've not handled your money well. Repent. Turn around and go the other way. Hiding from the guilt might drive you to spend even more.

HOW TO HANDLE CREDIT IN COLLECTIONS

Consider using a portion of your savings to pay off cards. Consider this: your savings may be paying one to five percent, while the credit card company is charging you 18-21 percent.

Borrow from 401-K. It makes a lot of sense to borrow from your 401-K to pay off a debt. The interest you will pay on the 401-K is much lower than that of a loan. The good thing about using your 401-K is that you will be repaying yourself with interest instead of paying interest to a finance company. Make sure you pay yourself back; failure to do so will cost you a 10 percent IRS penalty. In addition, you will be taxed as though the money you borrowed was normal income.

Negotiate with credit card companies. The enormous amount of credit card debt in this country has made creditors realize that if they don't want people backing down from their obligations completely (in other words, if they want to get ANY money back), they have to make deals. If you have debts in collection, you can:

Tell the company's collection department that you are having financial difficulties and need to have your minimum payment or the interest rate lowered, simple as that. They may say, "What can you manage?" You tell them the realistic amount you are able to pay. Believe God for favor with Him and the collection agency! When you catch up on delinquent payments, begin paying larger payments until you have paid it off.

If you are in a collection mode, write letters to each of your creditors acknowledging your inability to repay the debt due to limited income. Tell each one when you can begin repayment. They will appreciate your openness and honesty. In most instances, the creditor will be a lot nicer to you. Dealing with your situation honestly rather than hiding will help boost your bruised self-esteem.

While digging your way out of debt, you should continue to save, even if it's a small amount. Also, you must continue to give because the Bible promises it will be given back to you good measure, pressed down and shaken together and running over... shall men give unto you (Luke 6:38). God gave us a wonderful example of giving and receiving to get out of debt. He gave His Son Jesus to die for our indebtedness to sin so that He could have a big, righteous family. Today, God is still receiving from His giving. Again, when you give, your potential to receive is infinite.

Once you have followed these principles and have successfully retired your debt, commit yourself to living a debt-free life. A debt-free life is God's best for you. Remember, He said to,

> "Owe no man anything, except to love one another."
> —Romans 13:8 AMP

THE TRUE NATURE OF CREDIT CARDS

It seems to me that the American culture is deeply embedded in debt. Seemingly, we are a culture that is in love with credit and credit cards. In recent financial news reports, it is said that the average person has about $2,800 in credit card debt. The average household has credit card balances in excess of $7,500 and they are paying an average of 18 percent interest on their balance. This means they end up paying far more than the items are worth.

As believers move toward possessing God's wealth, it is more important than ever to break the habit of credit card spending. The best way to break the credit card habit is to simply cut them up and stop using them.

At bare minimum, you should have one credit card for emergency purposes or if there is a need to rent an automobile or book travel arrangements. If you are not capable of paying off your purchases as soon as the bill arrives, don't use the card! Instead, save money for that purchase.

The one card you retain in your possession should offer the lowest rate and the best terms you can find. A good credit card will have a reasonable interest rate and no annual fees. Before you agree to a new card, remember to read the fine print carefully. The fine print will give you important information on fees and rate changes. Master the basics of credit cards as outlined below and begin to live a debt-free life.

BASIC COMPONENTS OF CREDIT CARDS

Become knowledgeable of these components and concepts and begin to live a debt-free life!

> "And you will know the Truth, and the Truth will set you free."
>
> —John 8:32 AMP

The Truth refers to God and His Word. God's Word is Truth (John 17:17). When you handle money God's Way, you will get God's results—freedom!

Revolving Credit

Most credit cards offer revolving credit, meaning you can carry a balance from month to month. You will be required to make a small minimum payment each month. Revolving credit is how most companies make money—they profit by charging you interest on the balance you carry. If you use credit, be sure to pay off balances when your statement arrives.

Interest Rates

A credit card is a form of borrowing. As with any other loan, the privilege of borrowing does not come free. Cards come with either variable or fixed rates of interest. Although a fixed rate is usually a better idea, it is really a false attraction. Companies can change their terms at any time as long as they give customers 15 days notice. (That is one reason to make sure you read the inserts that come with your monthly bill).

Annual Percentage Rate (APR)
The APR is a yearly rate, expressed as a percentage. This represents your true cost of credit. Companies must reveal this rate on card agreements and your monthly account statements. You will also see a periodic rate, which is the rate applied to your monthly balance. These rates can change, so take note of them on your bills.

Introductory Rates
You may be tempted when an offer for a "pre-approved" credit card arrives in the mail. I get those envelopes all the time. You know. The envelope with "You've Been Approved" stamped across it in big red letters. Recently, I have been returning these letters back to the soliciting companies by writing NO THANKS on the offering letter and mailing the letter back to them in there postage paid envelope. Maybe, just maybe I will stop getting so many solicitation letters.

Be careful of cards offering an introductory rate! Many of these cards have a low "teaser" rate. However, those rates often last for only three to six months, after which the company hikes the rates right back up. Those rates often apply only to new purchases, not from balances you transfer to the new card.

In addition, many companies practice the classic bait-and-switch. Few people responding to the promise of a card with a 7.9 percent fixed rate will actually get approved for that rate. Keep in mind that the terms of your card are tied into your credit history. No one is going to give you anything but a high rate if your credit history is bad.

Balance Transfer
Balance transfer is the amount moved from one card to another card, usually in an attempt to get a lower interest rate.

Cash Advance

Cash you can borrow from your credit card company. You will have a cash advance limit, which will appear on your statement. Companies typically charge two percent or more of the total as a fee for the privilege. In addition to this access fee, a monthly interest rate is applied to the cash advance. This rate is usually higher than the rate applied to purchases.

Grace Period

The time period between making a purchase and being charged interest on that purchase. Grace periods, typically 25 days, have been shrinking to as little as 20 days, making it more difficult for even those who pay off their balances regularly to avoid interest charges. The grace period disappears if the cardholder already has a balance on the card.

Late Fees

This fee is charged for failure to make payments, on the presched-uled date. Some companies begin slapping on this fee as early as the date the bill is due. Late fees will generally cost $25 to $45 per occurrence, depending on the creditor. Some companies will arbitrarily increase your interest rate if you are consistently late because they now see you as a financial risk.

Inactivity Fees

Inactivity fees are the latest trick. Hard as it is to believe, companies are charging a fee on the average of $15 per month or more on customers who do not use their card frequently. This is probably because credit card companies are not making enough money off those of you who pay off balances regularly.

If you see such a fee, do not sit back and take it. Call your company and tell them you will not stand for it. They probably will wipe out the fee. Although they don't make much money off of you due to inactivity, they probably still want you as a customer just in case you screw up someday and run up a balance.

In conclusion, yes, there is life after debt. Even if you are overloaded with debt, you can dig yourself out by applying the spiritual and financial principles found in this book. These principles have been proven successful. Phenomenal spiritual and financial success can be yours—God's Way!

> "I am the Lord, who opens a way through the waters,
> making a path right through the sea."
> —Isaiah 43:16 TLB

Always remember, the world defines financial success as power, influence, money, and prestige; however, in the Christian world, true success is having an intimate relationship with the Heavenly Father. True success is doing that which is pleasing to the Father.

> "And whatever we ask we receive from Him, because
> we keep His commandments and do those things that
> are pleasing in His sight.
> —1 John 3:22 NKJV

Chapter 22
GOD'S MONEY-WISE NUGGETS!

Jesus had lots to say about money. More than half of His parables included discussions about money. Having said that, I believe it is important to become Money Wise! I would like to leave you with these paraphrased money-wise tips given by God on how to handle money:

Being wise is as good as being rich; in fact, it is better. (Ecclesiastes 7:11)

Those who love pleasure become poor; wine and luxury are not the way to riches. (Proverbs 21:17)

Work diligently and cheerfully at whatever you do. The Lord will give you an inheritance as your reward. (Colossians 3:23-24)

Greed causes fighting; trusting in the Lord leads to wealth. (Proverbs 28:2)

Do not steal. Do not cheat one another. Do not lie. (Leviticus 19:11)

Do not cheat or rob anyone. Always pay your hired workers on time. (Leviticus 19:13)

Beware. How much you own does not measure real life. (Luke 12:15)

Never begin a project until you count the cost. (Luke 14:28)

Wealth acquired dishonestly will not last. However, wealth from hard work grows. (Proverbs 13:11)

Do not be selfish or arrogant... Be humble, thinking of others as better than yourself. (Philippians 2:3)

The wise have wealth and luxury, but fools waste and spend whatever they get. (Proverbs 21:20)

Just as the rich rule the poor, so the borrower is servant to the lender. (Proverbs 22:7)

The wicked borrow and never repay, but the godly are generous givers. (Psalm 37:21)

God wants you to give what you have, not what you don't have. (2 Corinthians 8:12)

A person is a fool to store up earthly wealth but not have a rich relationship with God. (Luke 12:20-21)

Store your treasures in heaven, where they will never become moth-eaten or rusty and where they will be safe from thieves. (Matthew 6:20)

Do not labor to be rich. Riches are temporal. They
grow wings and fly away. (Proverbs 23:4-5)

Do not accept or demand bribes. (Proverbs 29:4; 17:23)

Wisdom or money can get you almost anything,
but only wisdom can save your life. (Ecclesiastes 7:12)

The servant who received the five bags of money
began immediately to invest money and doubled it.
(Matthew 25:16)

Do for others as you would like them to do for
you. (Luke 6:31)

Those who love money will never have enough.
(Ecclesiastes 5:10)

Be careful about borrowing. (Proverbs 22:7)

Be cautious about co-signing for others.
(Proverbs 17:18; 22:26)

Save for the future. (Proverbs 21:20)

Hard workers have plenty of food; playing around
brings poverty. (Proverbs 28:19)

It is important to become money wise. Take heed to the *Money-Wise Nuggets* your Heavenly Father has spoken through the Holy Spirit. Once you have obtained the wisdom on how to possess, preserve and distribute the wealth—wealth will come to you. Always remember, the wise have wealth and luxury, but fools spend whatever they get. (Proverbs 21:20)

My prayer for you is that you will walk in the overflow of God's financial, physical and spiritual wealth. I pray that the eyes of your understanding will be enlightened as you go and possess God's wealth. I also pray that you will give thought to and study the truth you have heard as you read these words of life.

> "The measure of [thought and study you give to the truth you hear] will be the measure [of virtue and knowledge] that comes back to you—and more [besides] will be given to you who hear."
>
> —Mark 4:24 AMP

EPILOGUE

Although this book focuses on financial wealth, I want you to know, the most precious gifts in this life are free. Money cannot buy those things which are priceless. What money cannot buy now, Jesus Christ can give freely without charge. He is the ultimate free gift.

If you do not have the free gift of salvation, you can receive right now. If you have never asked Jesus to come into your heart and be your Lord and Savior, you can do so right now. The Bible promises that when you pray the following prayer on the next page in faith, you will experience a new life in Christ...

PRAYER FOR SALVATION

Father, thank You for loving me so that You gave Your only begotten Son to die for my sins. I believe with my heart and say with my mouth that Jesus Christ, Your Son, is Savior and He is Lord. I believe You raised Jesus from the dead and He is alive.

I ask Jesus to come into my heart and be Lord and Savior of my life. Please forgive me for my sins and wash me new. Your Word said it is by grace through faith that I am saved.

I cannot do anything to earn salvation because it is Your free gift. I receive Your free gift right now and according to Your Word, I am saved, and I will spend eternity with You! Thank You Lord, I am saved! In Jesus Name, Amen!

Praise the Lord! You are now saved/born again and now you are a child of God!

Scripture References:

> "For God so loved the world, that he gave his only begotten Son, that whosoever believeth in him should not perish, but have everlasting life."
> —John 3:16

> "That if thou shalt confess with thy mouth the Lord Jesus, and shalt believe in thine heart that God hath raised him from the dead, thou shalt be saved."
> —Romans 10:9

> "For by grace are ye saved through faith; and that not of yourselves: it is the gift of God."
> —Ephesians 2:8

> "But as many as received him, to them gave he power to become the sons of God, even to them that believe on his name:"
> —John 1:12

If you have prayed this prayer, please write me and I will send you information on how to grow strong in the Lord. Write to:

rosegrant1@aol.com
or
Rose Grant Ministries
P.O. Box 48408
Oak Park, Michigan 48237

PRAYER FOR YOUR UN-SAVED LOVED ONE

Pray that their eyes will be opened so they can see how much God loves them.

Pray that they will be translated from the power of Satan to the power of God. Pray that they will be translated from darkness to light.

Pray for the Holy Spirit to send believers across their path to effectively share Jesus in such a way that they will not be able to resist the invitation to salvation.

Pray for ministering spirits (angels) to go and bring them into the Kingdom of God as they are heirs of salvation.

Pray that a fresh awareness of Jesus will live big in their hearts so they can serve Him all the days of their lives.

END NOTES

CHAPTER 10

1. John Waggoner, "MFS Settles Charges it didn't Broker Deals; Fund Company Pays $50M," *USA Today*, April 1, 2004, B05, Section: Money

CHAPTER 13

1. Forbes 2003 Financial Report, "Rich List 2003," *Forbes*, http://www.forbes.com/richlist2003/rich400land.html

CHAPTER 14

1. Forbes 2003 Financial Report, "Rich List 2003," *Forbes*, http://www.forbes.com/richlist2003/rich400land.html

About the Author

Rose Grant is a dynamic Evangelist commissioned by God to proclaim the truth and power of the Gospel of Jesus Christ with excellence and integrity. She is a licensed and ordained traveling minister, who is anointed to spread God's message that believers have total dominion in every area of life.

Rose's heartbeat is to win souls by ministering *"The Word of Truth"* to the lost. She also challenges Christians to grow spiritually, live victoriously and come to know the covenant-keeping God intimately.

Under the anointing of the Holy Ghost, Rose is an energetic preacher, motivational speaker, trainer and workshop facilitator for numerous faith-based organization and fortune 500 companies.

Her ministry gift has proven to be very effective in the spiritual, personal and professional development in the lives of those who hear her speak. The following are samples of satisfied clients:

Church Groups throughout the country
UAW General Motors
UAW Ford Motor Company
UAW DaimlerChrysler
Visteon Corporation
Delphi Automotive
Comerica Bank
Cornerstone University
Wayne State University
Westin Hotels

Rose is a former vice president of a major bank. She holds a Bachelor's Degree in Business Administration from Howard University. She has also had extensive studies in financial planning. She is a graduate of the Word of Faith Bible Training Center in Southfield, Michigan. Rose and her very loving and supportive husband Kyle, have two beautiful children, Kyla and Kyle II.

Reverend Grant is available for speaking engagements, conferences, workshops and seminars.

For more information, please contact us on
(313) 622-4219 or via fax (313) 387-4713
E-mail: RoseGrant1@aol.com
www.rosegrantministries.com